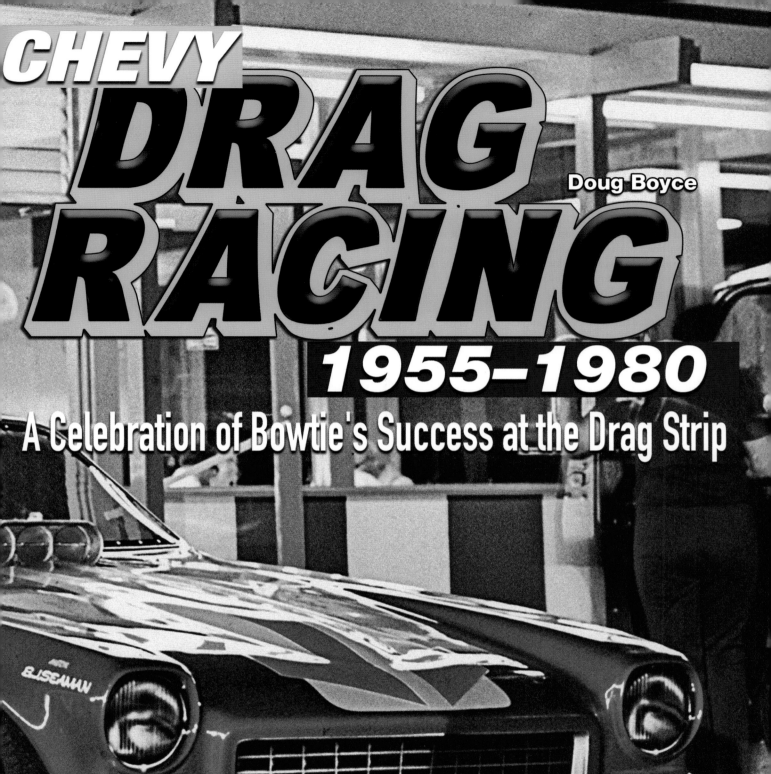

CHEVY DRAG RACING

1955–1980

A Celebration of Bowtie's Success at the Drag Strip

Doug Boyce

CarTech®

CarTech®, Inc.
838 Lake Street South
Forest Lake, MN 55025
Phone: 651-277-1200 or 800-551-4754
Fax: 651-277-1203
www.cartechbooks.com

Edit by Bob Wilson
Layout by Monica Seiberlich

ISBN 978-1-61325-499-8
Item No. CT659

Library of Congress Cataloging-in-Publication Data

Names: Boyce, Doug, author. | Cartech Inc.
Title: Chevy drag racing '55-1980 : a celebration of Bowtie's success at the drag strip / Doug Boyce.
Other titles: Chevrolet drag racing '55-1980
Description: Forest Lake, Minnesota : CarTech, Inc., 2020. | "Item No. CT659"–T.p. verso.
Identifiers: LCCN 2019042004 | ISBN 9781613254998 (Paperback)
Subjects: LCSH: Drag racing–United States–History–20th century. | Stock car racing–United States–History–20th century. | Chevrolet automobile. | Drag racers.
Classification: LCC GV1029.3 .B695 2020 | DDC 796.72–dc23
LC record available at https://lccn.loc.gov/2019042004

Written, edited, and designed in the U.S.A.
Printed in China
10 9 8 7 6 5 4 3 2 1

DISTRIBUTION BY:

Europe
PGUK
63 Hatton Garden
London EC1N 8LE, England
Phone: 020 7061 1980 • Fax: 020 7242 3725
www.pguk.co.uk

Australia
Renniks Publications Ltd.
3/37-39 Green Street
Banksmeadow, NSW 2109, Australia
Phone: 2 9695 7055 • Fax: 2 9695 7355
www.renniks.com

Canada
Login Canada
300 Saulteaux Crescent
Winnipeg, MB, R3J 3T2 Canada
Phone: 800 665 1148 • Fax: 800 665 0103
www.lb.ca

Contents

Acknowledgments

Joseph Agaman, Ed Aigner, John Banner, Tim Bass, Carl Bennett, John Bergener, Kevin Biermann, Forrest Bond, Bob Boudreau, Grady Bryant, Mike Bucher, Bob Callaham, Royce Chadwick, Mike Cochran, Todd Day, Gene Dunlap, Vickie Dunn, Bernard Durham, Dennis Ferrara, John Foster Jr., Royce Freeman, James Gipson, Ken Gunning, James Handy, Pat Hardy, Terry Hardy, Lou Hart, Daisy Hawkins, Lance Hill, Frank Iaconio, Charles Jacobs, Wayne Jesel, Chadly Johnson, Paul Johnson, Harry Kalwei, Jim Kampmann, Michael Keener, Kim Kimball, Dave Kommel, Bruce Larson, Bo Laws, Bob Martin, Dan Marvin, Brian McClanahan, Cal Method, Larry Morrison, Dan Napfel, Larry Nelson, Cotton Perry, Larry Pfister, Michael Pottie, Steve Reyes, Carl Rubrecht, Paul Sable, Robert Satmary Sr., Dale Schafer, Joe Scott, Bob Seibart, Tommy Shaw, Mike Strickler, Bob Snyder, Doug Thorley, Larry Tores, Allen Tracy, Eddie Vasquez Sr., Rick Voegelin, Bill White, George Whitney, Todd Wingerter, Bob Wood, Ray Zeller, and Richie Zul.

Dot Com Help...

Draglist, hotrod, cacklefest, competitionplus, NHRA, and your usual social media outlets.

Introduction

This book takes a celebratory look at the first 25 years of drag racing Chevys. From the mid-1950s, Chevrolet was and steadfastly remains the brand of choice for drag racers. Though there have been rewards for the manufacturer in every category, the main focus of this book is on those favored door cars and the categories where they did the most damage.

I need to say up front that although I grew up with a preference for Chevys, I've come to appreciate the on-track accomplishments of each of Detroit's brands. Props must be given to guys such as Sox & Martin, Dyno Don, and Bob Glidden, whose Hemis and Fords did their share of winning. These guys, and plenty of others, gave the Chevy racers fits. However, looking at the big picture, Chevy, or Chevy-powered cars, were the most prevalent. The stats and record books prove it.

With so many top-notch cars and racers, it was impossible to include them all. Try not to be too disappointed if you don't see your favorite or if so-and-so wasn't recognized. I gave a nod to those I thought were obvious and rounded it out with some of my personal favorites. To compile the stories herein, I hunted down as many people as I could to ensure accuracy. As a writer, there is nothing worse than publishing something and finding out some of the information was not as it should be. I'm no Sherlock Holmes, and for some of the features in this book I had no option but to rely on past interviews, previously written articles, and peers to get the story. Sadly, time marches on and has taken many greats to the big dragstrip in the sky.

"What about factory involvement?" you ask. We know Chevrolet supported the cause through June 1957 before GM's brass agreed to the Automobile Manufacturers Association's suggested ban on involvement and promotion of motorsports. Though it was never outright promoted after 1957, Chevy never completely abandoned the racers. It gave support through the backdoor and provided limited-production class killers. Think of the Z11 Impalas in 1963 or the ZL1 Camaro of 1969. Take a look at the parts; you don't need me to tell you that all those aluminum blocks, heads, forged pistons, and ropey solid-lift cams weren't designed for Mom and Pop's family bus. It wasn't until the 1980s that Chevrolet once more threw its support and dollars into the promotion of motorsports.

Chevrolet engineer Paul Van Valkenburgh, author of the 1972 book *Chevrolet—Racing? 14 Years of Raucous Silence! 1957–1970*, may have said it best, "If the (drag) racers think Chevrolet is actively or intentionally developing a winning product, it is because they grossly underestimate their own abilities." Chevy may have produced the goods, but it was up to the individual to make it a winner. It's for those more-than-capable drag racers that this book is written. It's through their efforts that Chevrolet remains drag racing's brand of choice 65 years later and into the future.

Shirley Muldowney had her share of success running her Double Trouble *Top Gas dragster through 1971. Twin 327 Chevy engines were built by her teenage son John. Additional assistance came by way of the* Freight Train's *John Peters, whose guidance helped Shirley's Chevys reach 200 mph. (Photo Courtesy Warren E. Case)*

Chapter One

The Building Blocks

There's no denying it, Chevy has always made great looking cars, although the 1960–1964 Corvair and the 1959 Chevy may be exceptions. Most of the bodystyles Chevy offered have been conducive to drag racing. Pick a class or a category and there is bound to be a car or engine combination to fit it.

Speaking of engines, let's go back to 1948 when Ford's flathead V-8 reigned supreme. Neither General Motors nor Chrysler had a mill that could touch it. Sure, a hopped-up Stovebolt inline-6 would occasionally give it a run for the money, but it was going to take a lot more to unseat the flathead, and in 1949 General Motors delivered. That year, both Cadillac and Oldsmobile introduced the over-

head valve (OHV) V-8. Do you think these guys had any idea about just what they had unleashed? I'm not talking about the effects it would have on ol' dad's status at the country club. I'm talking about the effect these new mills would have on the world of hot rodding. Almost overnight, technology had all but relegated the flathead to the dustbins of history. In 1955, there was a new king of the hill when Chevy introduced its own OHV V-8, an engine that made more power per inch than any engine had a right to make. In the following decades, the number one choice on the track would be a Chevy or Chevy power.

The Mighty Mouse

Many of you may have read the story on the birth of Chevy's V-8, but for those who haven't, here's the condensed version. Until 1955, the stodgy old six was the only choice for Chevy buyers. The winds of change began to blow at Chevrolet in 1952 with the hire of Ed Cole. General Manager Tom Keating tagged Cole to be his chief engineer and immediately put him to work designing the OHV V-8. Ed was not new to this by any means;

Chevy's rise to drag race supremacy began in 1955 with the release of the compact 265-ci. The little mouse that could maxed out at 400 ci in 1970. This 265-ci 162-hp version is saddled with luxury power steering, power brakes, and optional oil filter. (Photo Courtesy Tommy Lee Byrd)

he supervised the development of Cadillac's OHV V-8 a few years prior. The two men who joined Ed in development were Harry Barr (later chief engineer at Chevrolet) and E. H. Kelly as production engineer.

The agreed-upon design featured a 3.75 bore x 3.00 stroke, giving the engine 265 cubic inches. A lightweight valvetrain helped it peak at 5,600 rpm, which was a phenomenal number in the day when most stock V-8s were lucky to see 5,000 rpm. Further, the engine's short stroke reduced piston speed at higher RPM to allow for sustained high RPM operation. Ed Cole had touted that in testing the engine had been run at 5,600 rpm for 36 straight hours without failure.

The standard Turbo-Fire 265 developed 162 hp. Adding a Carter WCFB 4-barrel and dual exhaust upped that to 180 hp. Throw in the hotter, over-the-counter solid-lifer cam (0.404–0.413 lift) and horsepower climbed to 195. In a lightweight utility sedan, this engine cranked out 0–60 times in a little over 9 seconds, which easily outperformed engines of greater cubic inch displacement. The engine's compact size (approximately 28 inches long by 26 inches wide) and light weight of 530 pounds made it the engine swapper's delight. By the end of 1955, the engine was placed into everything from Fords to MGBs. Looking into its crystal ball, *Hot Rod* magazine stated in January 1956, "It seems that the popularity of the '55 Chevrolet V-8 is destined to assert itself on the pages of HRM at least once every 6 months." And it has.

The aftermarket immediately took to the engine, and with a few go-fast goodies, Frank McGurk was able to extract an additional 83 hp from the mill. He recorded a best of 14.03 in the quarter mile when he placed his engine in a utility sedan. The newly restyled '55 and its 265 were an instant success on the circle tracks. Herb Thomas, in his Smokey Yunick–prepared '55, earned

More than just a road racer, the V-8 Corvette with its fiberglass body and overall light weight proved to be the scourge of the NHRA Sport Production classes. This Virginia-based first-gen ran A/MSP with a healthy mouse motor and 4-speed. (Photo Courtesy Alan Garletts)

Tony Feil ran the gambit of Chevy drag cars, from Camaros to Corvettes, but he is probably best remembered for the work performed at his Tony Feil Performance Engines facility in Raritan, New Jersey. For decades, Tony's specialty was Chevy motors that found homes in everything from drag cars to drag boats. Tony was definitely one of the many unsung heroes who did his or her part to make Chevy number one. (Photo Courtesy Paul Sable)

Chevy its first ever superspeedway win at the Southern 500 in Darlington, and took 7 of the top 10 spots by defeating the Hemis and Rocket 88 Oldsmobiles driven by legendary names such as Fireball Roberts, Cotton Owens, and Lee Petty. The Chevys followed up on October 2 by winning Charlotte and again had 7 of the top 10 spots.

Without digressing too far, I need to mention Zora Arkus-Duntov, the man who brought the word *performance* into vogue at Chevrolet. Arkus-Duntov joined Chevy as an assistant engineer and is regarded as the father of the Corvette. His famed letter *Thoughts Pertaining to Youth, Hot Rodders, and Chevrolet,* penned shortly after he joined Chevrolet, guided the company's stance on performance for years to come. Until 1955, the Corvette was little more than a performance faux. Its bathtub-shaped fiberglass shell reeked of European styling, but its Blue Flame six and its 2-speed Powerglide transmission left a lot to be desired. It all changed in 1955

when Arkus-Duntov and Cole put their heads together and presented the V-8 Corvette. With the addition of the 4-speed transmission in 1957, the Corvette took a back seat to no one.

Chevy bumped the compression in 1956 and added a solid-lift cam (part number 3734077) and twin Carter carbs to boost power output to 240. Big changes came in 1957 when Chevy increased the bore of the 265 to 3.875 to produce 283 ci. Check out the performance options that kept Chevy on top in 1957:

- 283/283-hp fuel injection featuring a solid-lifter camshaft, domed pistons, and 10.5:1 compression
- 283/270-hp dual 4-barrel carburetors featuring the same solid-lifter camshaft as the 283-hp engine, flat-top pistons, and 9.5:1 compression
- 283/250-hp fuel injection featuring the same combination as the 270-hp engine with fuel injection and minus the solid lifters

In 1962, Chevy offered an over-the-counter kit for the Chevy II that enabled the hot rodder to ditch the weak-kneed 6- (or 4-) cylinder for a 265–283 or 327 V-8. More than a few went the fuel-injected 327 route and did plenty of damage in Factory Experimental. Dyno Don took his injected Chevy II wagon to B/FX class honors at the 1962 NHRA Winternationals. (Photo Courtesy Richard Nicholson)

- 283/245-hp dual 4-barrel carburetors featuring the same combination as the 270-hp engine minus the solid-lifter camshaft

For the next 15 years, the '55–'57 Chevys dominated drag racing's Stock classes, while the 283 fared pretty good no matter what it powered. Top Eliminator leaders, such as Pete Robinson and Chet Herbert, were boring and stroking the engine up to 450-plus inches. You couldn't get more bang for your buck; class wins and the record book proves it. By the time 1961 rolled around, 52 percent of all NHRA records were held by Chevys or Chevy-powered cars. It was a figure that only increased during the 1960s and was maintained into the 1970s.

In 1962, Chevy opened the 283 to 327 inches by increasing the bore to 4 inches and the stroke to 3.25. Produced through 1969, nearly every configuration of the engine from 250 to 350 hp was a Stock and Super Stock class winner. Those in Modified loved the engine, went to town, and came up with endless combinations by means of boring, stroking, and de-stroking. In 1976, Grumpy Jenkins bored out the 327 to 331 ci and pulled over 2 hp per inch. Jenkins won both the AHRA and NHRA Pro Stock world titles by running his engines in a pair of tube-chassis Monzas.

Rules back in the day gave every configuration a place to run. This injected small-block Chevy is a prime example of what you could find in any given Gas or Altered Tri-Five. Running Gas allowed for a 10-percent engine setback, whereas Altered allowed for a 25-percent setback. Every Chevy diehard knows those "camel hump" heads. (Author's Collection)

By 1976, Grumpy Jenkins was extracting over 2 hp of each inch of his 331. Helping the Monza to a record-setting 8.71 were modified 292 casting heads that sported 2.05 intake valves, a General Kinetics valve gear, and 660 Holleys on a much-modified Edelbrock intake. Final compression squeezed out to 14:1. (Photo Courtesy Lou Hart)

When it came to the drag car of choice, the '55–'57 Chevy was it. That is, until 1967 when Chevrolet introduced the Camaro. From bracket bombers to Funny Car, no single car has ever dominated the sport the way the Camaro has. Bob Frey, one of the most informed drag racing statisticians/historians, has come up with these amazing facts: as of 2019, 2,567 Camaros have been in the final round at the NHRA national events—of those, 1,260 were winners and 1,307 were runners-up; and 333 were 1969 Camaro winners—of those, 54 were Funny Car and 185 were Pro Stock winners. As I said, amazing. In the Camaro's debut year, Mike Fons drove his 396-ci 375-hp Super Stock Camaro to a runner-up finish at the World Finals. In 1968, Dave Strickler won the Super Stock World Championship with his Z28. Into the 1970s, Bobby Warren led the way and won three World titles with a string of Camaros.

With the introduction of the Camaro came a pair of new small-block options: the 302 and the 350. The 302 was only available in the Z28 and had a short life span that lasted from 1967 through 1969. Rated by the factory

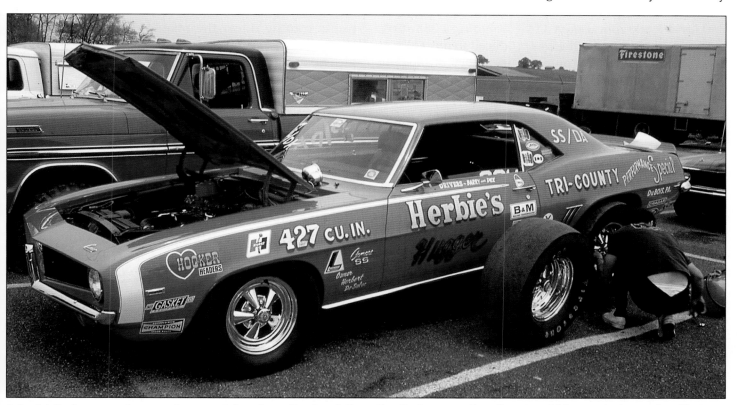

I doubt that any car has made more trips down the track than the first-generation Camaro. This one belonged to Herb DeSalve and was driven by his son Barry, who won the Division 1 S/S title in 1971. As well as set class records, Barry won class at every national event he entered between 1969 and 1972. Times in the 10.70s were the norm for the L89-powered SS/DA car. (Photo Courtesy Michael Mihalko)

Chevrolet only produced the 255-hp 350 through April 1969, and Bud Rowe had to trek to Virginia from his home in North Carolina to find a dealer with one in stock. "I let the dealer keep the wheels and tires and put the slicks on right at the dealership. I hauled the car home, pulled the engine, blueprinted it, and the first big race was Indy." (Author's Collection)

at 290 hp, the NHRA immediately refactored the engine to 315. Actual dyno pulls showed the engine produced 350 hp at 7,000 rpm. Derived by combining a 283 stroke with a 327 bore, the engine was produced to meet SCCA's Trans Am cubic inch requirements. Chevy stuffed the engine with the best of parts: 2.02 heads, an aluminum high-rise intake, Holley 800 cfm, 11.0:1 compression, and a solid-lifter camshaft from the 1964–1965 fuel-injected 327 that featured 0.452 intake/0.455 exhaust lift.

From a performance perspective, the original small-block peaked at 350 inches in 1967 when Chevy increased the stroke to 3.48 inches. Though the horsepower rating maxed out at 370 in 1970, the LM1 255-hp engine of 1969 was the choice of the nation's Stock and Super Stock racers. It was an underrated engine equipped with a Rochester Quadrajet carb, 1.94 heads, 9.0:1 compression, and a cam with 0.390/0.410 lift. The engine was killer in class, proven by North Carolina's Bud Rowe. Bud was the first to bring attention to the LM1 when he won I/S with his Nova at the Nationals in 1969 and set the class record in the process with a 12.86.

W-Series Engines

Next in block development was the 348, which debuted in 1958 inside an all-new, wider, longer, and heavier Fisher body. Born out of necessity, the W-series engine served a purpose and was a stepping stone to the Mark IV big-block introduced in 1965. Looking into its

crystal ball, Chevy knew it was going to need a bigger engine with more torque to handle the bigger cars and trucks coming down the pike. The small V-8 with its short stroke, thus limited torque, wasn't going to make it. The W-series featured combustion chambers built into the block and a 74-degree deck, as opposed to the small-block and big-block deck angle of 90 degrees. The heads were topped with W-shaped rocker covers.

Although the 348 held its own when the Stockers ran, the engine never really caught on the way the small-block did due to a number of reasons: its additional 140 pounds of weight, the greater external dimensions, and its limited RPM (Chevy recommended a 5,400 limit). The 348 featured a 4.48 bore-to-bore centerline that gave approximately 3/4-inch spacing between cylinders, leaving plenty of room to open up its 4.125 bore to 4.132 in 1961 to provide 409 ci. Horsepower for the 348 peaked in 1961 at 350.

The 409 was an immediate hit in the Stock ranks when Dyno Don Nicholson opened the 1961 drag racing season by winning the NHRA Winternationals. Nicholson Impala recorded a 13.25 to defeat the Chevy Biscayne of Frank Sanders in the Top Stock final. In 1962, Nicholson repeated with a 409-ci 409-hp Bel Air, and Hayden Proffitt took the Nationals that year with a similarly equipped Bel Air.

Horsepower was increased from 409 to 425 in 1963, but the big news was the release of the limited run of

Bill Jenkins gained a reputation in 1961 when he teamed with Dave Strickler on a record-holding 409-powered Biscayne. Strickler's Old Reliable 1962 Bel Air ran a Jenkins-prepped 409 to win SS/S class at Indy with a 12.97 at 113.35 mph. (Photo Courtesy Mike Strickler)

50 (or so) Z11 Impalas. The cars featured 147 aluminum parts, and a W-series engine measuring 427 ci lived under the lightweight hood. Twin Carter AFB carbs, an aluminum two-piece intake, a solid-lifter cam with 0.556/0.556 lift and 325 duration, improved heads with 2.19 intake and 1.72 exhaust valves, and 13.5:1 compression gave the mill its rated 430 hp at 6,000 rpm. The Impalas dominated action in 1963 when Frank Sanders and Dave Strickler won national events. With the emergence of the

The 1963 Z11 427 was an all-out race engine and had the most-feared block on the scene. Frank Sanders took Limited Production with this one at the NHRA Winternationals, while Dave Strickler won Little Eliminator at the Nationals. (Author's Collection)

match race Funny Car in 1964, many of these 427s found their way into Chevelles and Chevy IIs to defeat their share of factory-backed Fords and Mopars.

The Biggest Blocks

The 396 debuted in 1965 and gained its "semi-hemi" nickname due to its canted-valve design. The engine was an evolution of the W-series design and featured the same bore spacing, side oiling, and valve diameter. The new design, with its combustion chambers back in the head, greatly improved volumetric efficiency. Bore and stroke measured 4.094 x 3.760. The 325-hp and 375-hp versions of the engine inside a first-gen Camaro proved to be a sensation in Super Stock.

Chevy opened the bore of the 396 to 4.25 in 1966 and provided 427ci. The performance option codes read like alphabet soup: L68, L71, L72, L88, L89, and ZL1 with horsepower ratings up to 425. Goodies ranged from 850 Holleys to 12.5:1 compression. On the track, the winning combos prove to be too many. How about the 425-hp L72-powered Biscaynes of 1966 or the L72-powered 1968 Camaro? Rated at 425 hp, the L72 featured nothing but the best: a forged crank, aluminum pistons, 11.0:1 compression, a 0.520 solid-lift cam, high-rise aluminum intake, and 780 Holley carburetor. With the simple addition of slicks and headers, the Camaro was an 11-second performer. Bill Jenkins, Dick Harrell, Ed Hedrick, and Kelly Chadwick made the car an instant winner.

Pro Stock rule changes in 1982 saw the NHRA go with a 500-ci maximum, 2,350-pound minimum. No surprise here, the big-block Chevy led the way. At the season-opening Winternationals, 7-second times ruled the day, and in the final round, Frank Iaconio (seen here in 1983) defeated Lee Shepherd. (Photo Courtesy Steve Reyes)

When it came to body choices, the options were unlimited to the Chevy racer. The early Stovebolt Chevys made great Gassers and later bracket bombers. Future five-time Top Fuel world champ Joe Amato made a name for himself while campaigning this 1940 Chevy, first in Modified Production and then in BB/GS. Power was supplied by a blown big-block Chevy. (Photo Courtesy Michael Mihalko)

Chevy released the 427-ci late in 1965, and in short order the hot rod fraternity began working its magic. Demar Ray, a master machinist and engine builder with Cragar, got ahold of the engine that fall and added a 1/4-inch stroke to it to come up with 454 ci. This Demar build resides in the King Kong Anglia of the Kohler brothers and recorded low-9 times. Cragar supplied the supercharger, manifold, and drive combination, while Hilborn furnished the injection and pump. (Photo Courtesy Carlos Cedeno)

Chadwick and Harrell were two of the guys who used the tall-deck version of the 427 in Funny Car. The block allowed for a longer stroke and was a popular choice into the early 1970s for those who ran a Chevy engine in Funny Car and Top Fuel.

Stroking the 427 to an even 4 inches in 1970 gave 454 ci and was Chevy's last performance engine of the muscle car era. The engine was loaded with the best parts Chevy's high-performance bin had to offer: 11.25:1 compression, 2.19 valves, a 0.520 solid-lift cam, and an 800 Holley carburetor. Although the externally balanced engine was the king of the street in 1970 with its 450 hp and 500 ft-lbs of torque, its on-track success and popularity was limited. There were a number of rea-sons for that, including the cost of buying a new Chevelle or Corvette (the only cars you could get with the engine), and possibly an unfavorable weight versus factored horsepower rating. Drag racers were always looking for the least-expensive car to run that fell closest to the low end of the weight break. The few LS6 cars that did appear did not disappoint. Truppi-Kling found an ideal home for its LS6 powered ragtop in SS/EA. Thought to be a class that only a Mopar could win, the team dominated and won national events and set the class record. Bernie Agaman did the same in the mid-1970s with his low-compression Corvette in SS/CA. These two 454 cars alone were enough to rewrite history and ensure that the engine's on-track accomplishments aren't soon forgotten.

Harold Ramsey was crowned the NHRA's first Stock points champ and took Super Stock in 1959 with his '57 Chevy at the NHRA Nationals held in Detroit. Ramsey's 150-series '57 was powered by a slightly warmed-over fuel-injected 283 backed by a 3-speed transmission. It turned a 14.94 at 92.30 mph. (Photo Courtesy Jack Bleil)

Chapter Two

Boss of the Stocks

Starting in 1955 when the NHRA held its first Nationals event, there were only four Stock classes on the books. As was the case, the car closest to the light end of the class weight break had a better chance of winning. The class breaks in 1955 were pretty wide, ranging from 2 to 6 pounds per cubic inch, and it was the smart person who chose his or her entry wisely.

By the time 1960 rolled around, Stock had grown to seven classes and the breaks had somewhat tightened. The rules at the time limited mods to uncapped exhaust and cheater slicks no wider than stock. But as the 1960s unfolded, rules loosened considerably and the popularity of Stock grew. Eventually classes ranged from A through Z. Through the 1960s, close to 75 percent of cars on the nation's dragstrips were Stockers, with 75 percent of those being Chevys. With the number of body/drivetrain combinations that Chevy offered, it's really no surprise that it maintained its lead for decades.

1964 NHRA Nationals

Before the NHRA Nationals in 1964, the lower Stock classes didn't have their own Eliminator program. Racers ran for class and that was it. The Eliminators were reserved for the Top Stocks and gave rise to guys such as Don Nicholson, Hayden Proffitt, and Dave Strickler, who from 1961 through 1963 dominated action with their 409-powered Chevys, winning four of the six NHRA National events.

At the Nationals in 1964, the big Chevy winner in Junior Stock was Michigan's Phil Chisholm. As a member of the Dick Griffin–led Chevair Race Team, Phil and his 327-ci 250-hp I/SA 1964 Bel Air wagon overcame a field of approximately 306 cars to meet and defeat Chevair teammate Jon Callender in his 1959 Biscayne in the

Bruce Morgan Goes Undefeated

The stock points champion in 1961 was Bruce Morgan with his B/Stock fuel-injected '57 Bel Air. Bruce purchased the black beauty new in 1957 from Calliau Chevrolet in Pasadena. He raced the car every spare moment and spent a few bucks having the 283 worked over and dyno tuned by "Dyno Don" Nicholson, the future Ford-Mercury standout. Reportedly, the 283 had the factory 10:5.1 slugs replaced with 1960–1961 Corvette 11:1 pistons. It's something the teardown barn obviously never picked up on at the Nationals in 1961 when Bruce took Stock honors. In a feat that I doubt has ever been repeated, Bruce finished the season undefeated. Amazing is the fact that he drove the Bel Air every day and to every event he attended. The '57 was sold at the end of the season and Bruce semi-retired to his trucking job.

Bruce Morgan met and defeated Richard Hilt for Top Stock honors at the 1961 NHRA Nationals. Though Hilt crossed the finish line first, he was later disqualified on a valvetrain technicality. (Author's Collection)

Though the all-new Chevy in 1958 looked great, bigger didn't equate to being better, at least not on the track. An optional 250-hp fuel-injected 283 and a 315-hp 348 kept the car competitive on a local level. (Photo Courtesy Bill Truby)

"Honest Jon" Callender defeated Bill Spanakos in the finals at the 1965 Nationals with a 15.29. Those were not bad times for a 185-hp 283 Biscayne that weighed more than 3,500 pounds. (Photo Courtesy Forrest Bond)

At the 1963 NHRA Winternationals, the Z11 Impalas were forced to run Limited Production/Stock after Chrysler, the race sponsor, complained that the cars did not fit Super Stock class. Arizona's Frank Sanders was initially crowned the LP/S class winner. Frank's Z11 was reported to be the first to top 120 mph. Frank went on to attain the number one position on the Drag News Top Stock Eliminator list, winning 19 of 20 races. (Author's Collection)

final with a 15.47 at 87.63 mph. The Chevairs fielded six Stockers at the Nationals; all but one were Chevys, and all six won their respective class. Callender returned to Indy in 1965 to win the Nationals and defeated the '55 Chevy of Bill "Spyder" Spanakos.

Monster Mash

The two *Monster Mash* '55 Chevys, probably the most-feared Stockers of all time, may have belonged to Bill and Andy Spanakos, but they were all Grumpy Jenkins. During the 1960s, Jenkins turned building Stockers into a science, and he used every trick in his book on the *Monster Mash* cars, especially the second one. Spyder grabbed the I/Stock record in May 1965 at Cecil County, turning a 14.19 at 95.64 mph, although the *Monster Mash II* was capable of running 13.30 times.

Jenkins and the Spanakos brothers were always reluctant to discuss the modifications made to the *Monster Mash II*, but I had the opportunity to discuss the car with Spyder, Jenkins, and the preceding owners. This car was one trick piece. Starting with the body, Spyder purchased a well-worn former Bell Telephone utility sedan. It was the lightest of the '55s and wasn't weighed down with such frivolous items as a rear seat and insulation. The car was made even lighter by Jenkins and Spyder by removing everything they deemed to be dead weight, including wiring to the horn, wipers, and some lights. Further, every other nut and bolt in the car was replaced with aluminum, and all the bolts had the extra length cut off. The cast factory grille was replaced with lightweight conduit from a TV antenna. The inner front fenders were

Bill Spanakos in the first Monster Mash *is seen here at Maryland's Mason Dixon during a 1963 match against the C/Highway (Gas) '55 of Don "Mac" McIlvaine and Ray Hagee. Both cars were prepared by Bill "Jiggs" Jenkins. (Photo Courtesy Michael Bellano)*

sandblasted, and to get the required minimal weight back into the car and onto the right end, the rear inner quarter panels were coated with lead.

Stock class rules of the day dictated a maximum of 7-inch slicks, so to harness the estimated 370 hp, the body mounts were hogged out and the body was slid back on the frame as far as possible. Tom Drabik, who owned the car after it retired from racing, had to replace

> **"She didn't like racing, so I sold the car. Jenkins hit the roof– I never saw him so mad. Tools were flying everywhere."**
> – Bill "Spyder" Spanakos

the left rear quarter panel on the car. "The new panel had the wheel wells in a different place than the ones on the panel we cut out," he said. The stock rubber body-mount biscuits were replaced with mounts from a 1960 Chevy that were reported to be an inch taller. This raised the car's center of gravity, which (back then) was believed to aid traction.

When it came to the suspension, the rear end rode on fabricated mounts, and up front, A-arms were fabricated with a combination of stock '55 arms and 1958 Chevy parts. Jack Arnew, a friend of Jenkins, made a jig for the custom upper A-arms, which moved camber and ensured the wheels stayed straight all the time.

The heart of the potent 265 was the blueprinted camshaft. According to Jenkins, "Chevrolet's own 195-hp service camshaft (part number 3711354) for the 265 wouldn't meet its own specifications by a considerable amount. We took the specifications given to the NHRA and made camshafts to those specs." It was through long-time friend George Linton that Jenkins was able to get Ed Winfield to grind the new cams for him. George, an old Pennsylvania racer, had relocated to Hayward, California, where he befriended Winfield.

Jere Stahl, who was tight with Jenkins, recalled, "Two of those cams being the 3711354 and the Duntov 3736097 cam, Bill turned those cams over to Sig Erson to have precise copies made. At the same time, Sig Erson would cast or stamp the factory casting number into them. The Winfield/Sig Erson cams were good for 1½ to 2 mph." The only ones who could get their hands on one of these blueprinted cams were customers of Jenkins or Stahl. Former Jenkins Competition employee Charlie

The original Monster Mash Chevy, pictured here at York US-30 was wrecked in a towing accident around 1965. The second Monster Mash was discovered in 2018, in remarkable condition, languishing in an Ohio garage. It will see a full restoration. (Photo Courtesy John Durand)

Strunk recalled, "The cams opened and closed the valves much faster than factory cams."

Further, Charlie said that they had to either pin the rocker studs or run screw-in studs to keep them from pulling out of the heads. "There were heads available from Chevrolet as replacements that were far better than the originals. We got about 30 of them in one time and picked the best 4 and sent the rest back. I was able to enlarge the ports by machining the area below the seats and making it look factory. Just by doing a little work with a grinder that was unnoticeable helped a lot. Since the NHRA tech checked the valve spring tension, the best thing you could do was to lighten the valves. I spent many hours making the valves lighter and thinner but keeping them looking stock. This was followed up with a nice three-angle valve job."

Jenkins was fanatical when it came to ensuring that each cylinder received the same air/fuel mixture and spent a lot of after-hours time toying with carbs and intakes. "He would put grooves under the carb and jet each of the four barrels different. That was all his thing, and he rarely talked about it."

Backing the engine was a slick-shifted Saginaw 3-speed transmission that housed lower NASCAR gears. The rear end housing carried 4.56 gears and rode on fabricated perches. Gear oil was replaced with 10w30, whereas the carrier and axle bearings ran thicker grease.

The '55 dominated East Coast Stocker action into 1966, holding the class record for two years. It all came to an end when Spyder got married. "She didn't like racing,

so I sold the car. Jenkins hit the roof—I never saw him so mad. Tools were flying everywhere." Though the second *Monster Mash* car survives, and of this writing is waiting on someone to restore it, the first one passed through a few hands before the well-worn racer was finally sent to the scrapyard.

The Wenzel Brothers

With an explosion in Stock class participation, the NHRA divided the category in 1967 and created a new Super Stock category for the Top Stocks. Chevy again ruled

Smiles were all around the Wenzel camp after winning the 1967 Nationals. From left to right are Shaker engineers who helped prep the Camaro: Omar Lozo, Herb Brinn, and Ron Kindell. Each enjoy the moment with Ben and Dave Wenzel. (Author's Collection)

Wayne Jesel and the *Yoo-Hoo Too*

Not meaning to hammer on today's youth, but I can't imagine many of today's 15-year-olds doing what Wayne Jesel was doing on a sweltering August day in 1965. After consulting with header guru Jere Stahl on the best choice of car around to build a Junior Stocker, Wayne picked up a '56 sedan delivery. Wayne was busy with the sandblaster outside of the Jesel & Smith shop, which was located to the rear of Duffy's in Red Bank, New Jersey, after he stripped the body and pulled it from the chassis. This is the kind of detail prep many Stock racers put into their cars if they wanted to win.

The body was sprayed a Cadillac fire mist gold with Cadillac fire mist red stripes to match the colors of sponsor Yoo-Hoo, the chocolate drink. Jesel's partner, Tony Massari's father, was on the board of directors of Yoo-Hoo and set up an appointment for the boys to make a pitch. It must have been quite the pitch because they walked out with a $2,500 deal in what was reported to be the first non-automotive paid drag racing sponsorship.

For power, the delivery relied upon a 225-hp mill. Go-fast features included twin Carter WCFB 4-barrel carburetors, 9.25:1 compression, and a blueprinted 077 cam. Aftermarket aid came from Stahl, Jack Merkel, and Vitar transmissions who prepared the Hydra-Matic transmission. The *Yoo-Hoo Too* proved to be one of the fastest GSA cars in the nation. It turned a record 14.33 time and took class at both the AHRA and NHRA Springnationals as well as the NHRA Nationals. Between 1966 and 1967, Jesel reset the class record five different times, and both years finished second in Division 1 points.

The delivery took on many forms through 1971, and it was later transformed into a wagon to better conform to revised NHRA rules. After 1971, the wagon was sold to some place now long lost to memory.

The sand flies as Wayne Jesel blasts away 10 years of grime from the sedan delivery, soon to be the *Yoo-Hoo Too*. Once clean, the underside was painted white while the frame was coated black. As a no-cost means of improving rear weight bias, the body would be slid back as far as possible on the frame mounts. (Photo Courtesy Wayne Jesel)

The *Yoo-Hoo Too* is believed to have been the very first Hydra-Matic-equipped, Stock-class sedan delivery built. Initially, partner Tony Massari did the driving because the pair's home track of Englishtown had a rule that said no one younger than 18 was allowed in the pits. Sixteen-year-old Wayne missed the cutoff; although, occasionally the Natt brothers (track owners) would turn a blind eye. (Photo Courtesy Wayne Jesel)

Still knocking them out 50-plus years on. The Wenzel brothers' Camaro gets it done these days in 10.40 seconds. This "Zapper" has been a drag car from day one. (Photo Courtesy Rebecca Ledford)

the roost in Stock with Ben and Dave Wenzel and their 1967 Camaro Z28 that won the Nationals and "Little" George Cureton in his '56 sedan delivery that won the NHRA World Championship. The Wenzels' win at the Nationals and Grumpy Jenkins's win in Super Stock were the first major victories for the all-new Camaro.

The Wenzels ran Chevys since 1963 and were convinced to buy their Camaro from friends at Shaker Engineering. Ben said, "I initially had my mind set on a 375-hp Chevelle, seeing the success Booth-Arons enjoyed with theirs, and the fact I had my clock cleaned the year before by the Chevelle of Odus Rigsby." The Nationals win is still a highlight for Ben, as he recalled it was a tough go, beating the Gunning Brothers' Chevy in the final with a 12.33.

Still running the Camaro today, Ben and Dave have two NHRA National event wins, two runners-up, two IHRA national wins, and countless Eliminator-round wins under their belt with no regrets having chosen the Camaro.

"Little George" Cureton

At the World Finals in 1967, George Cureton combined his fantastic driving abilities with a Jenkins Competition–built 225-hp 265 to defeat Wally Nisson in Gus Phillipich's '56 Chevy wagon. George's '56 *Tokyo Rose*

continuously ran sub-record times and was regularly protested by its competitors. As George recalled, at $50 a pop, he made a bundle of money, as the car always proved legal. Backing the potent little 265 was a Freddie Borcherdt–prepared 4-speed Hydra-Matic transmission. The bulletproof Hydra-Matic with its favorable gear ratios were a contributing factor in the domination of the Tri-Five sedan deliveries during this period in drag racing.

George followed his World Championship victory by winning the LSA class at the Nationals in 1969. He parted with the delivery shortly after that and tried his hand in a fuel-injected Pontiac. George's success continued well into the 1970s and started with the purchase of Bobby Warren's NHRA World Finals–winning Chevy Nova in 1970. George took possession of the car, minus the 4-speed transmission, immediately after Warren's World Champ win. George ran the Nova in K/SA during 1971 and earned the Division 1 points championship—his second title in three years.

After a brief retirement, George purchased Garley Daniels's SS/O 1966 Chevy II. "I saw the car run at the 1976 Summernationals at Englishtown. When he beat Buddy Ingersol's factory-backed Olds with his little 283 Nova, I knew it would be a killer car with the Powerglide

"Little George" Cureton's Tokyo Rose could run under the 13.2, L/SA class record all day long, thanks to a Jenkins Competition–built, 225-hp 265. The delivery's name came with the original red paint. (Photo Courtesy Michael Mihalko)

> **When [Garley Daniels] beat Buddy Ingersol's factory-backed Olds with his little 283 Nova, I knew it would be a killer car with the Powerglide in SS/OA. The car wasn't for sale, but I convinced Garley to sell it."**
> – **"Little George" Cureton**

in SS/OA. The car wasn't for sale, but I convinced Garley to sell it. On August 13, 1976, I flew down to Grantsboro, North Carolina, and picked up the car hauler and the Nova. I raced the car until 1983 and sold it to Ned Smith in Jessup, Georgia, after that year's Gators. Garley had maintained my motors during most of that period. He was one truly smart man and could make ungodly amounts of horsepower legally."

"Little George" had his share of success with the ex–Garley Daniels Chevy II. The car would be a killer in SS/OA with engines by Daniels. (Photo Courtesy George Whitney)

From 1968–1969 Car Craft *magazine captured the hearts of many with their "How to Build the Ultimate Junior Stock" series. Readers followed the six-part series as Joe Allread meticulously prepared the fuel-injected wagon for J/S competition. The wagon would run a record setting 12.86 and a best of 12.63 mph. (Author's Collection)*

Now isn't this a Tri-Five Chevy lover's dream. Starting on the top left are Brad Watkins and Alex Jarrell; on the bottom, Jay and Buck Wheatley. Wheatley's hauling supplied the truck that took this group to Indy in 1968. (Photo Courtesy Michael Mihalko)

George used the car to set the class record four different times. He won one national event (the 1979 Summernationals), was runner up at another, and took class at national events a total of eight times before finally retiring from racing.

Dave Boertman

An emerging star in 1967 was Dave Boertman, who was getting it done behind the wheel of a 1959 Chevy Biscayne. He won the NHRA World Championship in 1968 to extend Chevy's run of Stock World Championships to five in a row. Dave's *Budget Breaker*, aptly named due to its habit of breaking parts (Dave joked he spent more time under the car than in it) was powered by a 185-hp 283, 4-speed combination.

At the World Finals, Dave's 15.10 ET was enough to hold off the handicapped charge of Bill Izykowski's 427-powered 1966 Biscayne. Dave ran his Biscayne through 1969 before NHRA rule changes for the coming season made his combination obsolete.

Aptly named Budget Breaker *due to its tendency to break every part imaginable. Looking back, Dave said he spent more time under the Biscayne than in it. "I was going through axles, U-joints, and center hangers like crazy." The Biscayne would be powered by a 185-hp 283 backed by a 4-speed. (Photo Courtesy Dale Schafer)*

Happy days for the Boertmans as Dave makes it two in a row, winning Indy in 1970 after winning the Summernationals. The 255-hp 350 propelled the 1969 Biscayne to an N/SA record of 13.48. (Author's Collection)

After watching Bud Rowe's 255-hp 350-powered Nova compete at the NHRA Nationals in 1969, Dave knew what his next car was going to be. After checking the specifications and his options regarding body choices, he settled on a 1969 Biscayne. It was a combination that fit perfect in N/S.

"I knew watching Bud and checking the specs on this engine, this thing would fly." Dave's new Biscayne was an ex-police car that had been stolen at one point and driven into Michigan's Grand River by thieves. Dave counted on Tom Elk to build the 0.025-over engine for the new car that later set the N/SA national record in May 1970 with a 13.69 at 99.66 mph. Wins at both the NHRA Summernationals and Nationals followed, as well as another division crown, which was Dave's third in a row.

TRW pistons and a General Kinetics dual-pattern camshaft filled the mouse motor. Cylinder heads were milled 0.015 to meet the minimal 73.26-cc combustion chambers. A turbo 350 transmission with a 9-inch convertor and a 12-bolt rear end carrying 5.13 gears backed the 350.

By the end of the year, the Biscayne's 255 hp was refactored to 270. It was no problem for Dave, as the car could run 3/10 under the class record. Dave left the Chevys behind in 1971 when Gil Kirk of the Rod Shop came calling. Kirk wanted to lock in a Chrysler multi-car deal and was told the only way it was going to happen was if he landed Boertman. Dave discovered this after the fact. "I guess I had been a big enough pain in their butts that it was a way of eliminating me."

The Final Go for Junior Stocks

It seems appropriate that when the NHRA made sweeping changes to Stock eliminator at the end of 1971, the final two cars standing at the season-ending Supernationals were a pair of Tri-Five Chevys. Through the 1960s, the '55–'57 Chevy dominated the category to the point that the NHRA changed the format, eliminating the cars from competition.

Paul Ditcher and partner Keith Berg hold the distinction of winning the final Stock eliminator under the then-existing rules. The pair joined forces midway through the season. Paul supplied a '55 Bel Air and Keith, who usually ran an early 1950s Olds, financed the venture. Their final-round opponent was Val Hedworth and his 150-series '56 wagon.

To reach the final, the two cars had to wade through a 32-car field. With confidence in Paul's driving abilities, or maybe just a little arrogance, Keith approached Val prior to the final run and offered to split the winnings with him. Val had no interest in that; and besides, he had no clue as to what made Keith think they were going to win. In the end, the final proved anticlimactic, as overeager Val and his O/SA wagon lit the dreaded red bulb. Paul reset the R/S record on the final run with a 13.90 at 96.77 mph. Not that it mattered because in 1972, all Stock records were erased when the NHRA went to a pure stock format. In the process, they implemented a 10-year

It's the 1971 season-ending Supernationals and the final race of Stock Eliminator before the NHRA moved to a Pure Stock format. Paul Dilcher, driving the Berg & Dilcher R/S '55 took the win after Division 7 points champion, Val Hedworth, in his 225-hp '56 Chevy wagon drew the dreaded redlight. Lessening the pain of the loss was the fact Val built the engine for Dilcher. Val again took the Division 7 points championship in 1972. (Author's Collection)

rule that eliminated any car older than 1963. It was a move welcomed by Detroit's Big Three. They were in the market of selling new cars and were tired of the Tri-Five Chevy's domination. As the new decade unfolded, the NHRA relaxed the rules to the point that by the latter half of the 1970s, the cutoff had settled on 1960. In 2015, the Tri-Fives were once again welcomed back into the fold.

Cal and Mary Ann Method

Washington state's Cal Method is one of many who survived the NHRA purge of Stock Eliminator in 1971. Cal more than survived; between him and his wife Mary Ann, who started racing in 1976, they set something in the neighborhood of 150–200 class records. Cal became serious about drag racing back in 1964 with a 1961 Impala powered by a 283 2-barrel. From there it was a step up with a fuel-injected, 9-passenger '57 station wagon. He ran the wagon through 1967, set the F/S record, and won his first points meet in Edmonton, Canada, with it.

In 1968, the motor was pulled and dropped into a sedan delivery in front of a Hydra-Matic transmission.

The Hydramatic gave Cal nightmares until he had British Columbian Jim Mannel go through it.

"I made my first run at the Nationals in 1969, and when I got back to my trailer, there were probably 25 guys there wanting to know who built my transmission." At the same race, Cal was approached by a lady who wanted to buy the car for her 16-year-old son. "I didn't want to sell, as I loved the car. I spent 1,000 hours on body and paint and was seeing some success with the car." It was a good combination that took Cal to the finals at the 1968 Winternationals where a tired transmission saw him come up short.

Come 1971, changing rules made the Hydra-Matic in the delivery an illegal combination, thus rendering the car obsolete. Cal parted the car out. He sold the motor to a circle-track racer and built himself a 1965 Chevelle wagon, powered by a 283 and 4-speed. Cal ran the Chevelle for about six months before he built a 1966 Impala. That same year, Cal won his first division crown.

The Impala started Cal on a run of full-size Chevys that brought him most of his class records and wins well into the 1980s. Chevy wagons, two-doors, and four-

Cal Method established his reputation behind the wheel of this great-looking sedan delivery. Cal stated that they put 1,000 hours into body and paint, and kind of patterned the fade after John Diana's '56 delivery. (Photo Courtesy Vern Scholz)

The Methods' strategy for winning was to use the under-rated 283 in disposable bodies ranging from Chevelle wagons to full-size two-doors, four-doors, and wagons. Check the record books, the Methods owned O, P, Q, and R/Stock by simply swapping bodies, drivetrains, and intake/carburetor combos. (Photo Courtesy Cal Method)

Talk about getting the most bang for your buck. The Methods wore out a few full-size Chevys over the years, exchanging bodies as quick as some changed socks. A 275-hp 327 saw this 1966 running G/S in the mid-1970s. (Photo Courtesy Cal Method)

doors of the mid-1960s vintage filled the Methods' yard as Cal ran nearly every combination imaginable. "Back when they gave you points for the record, I would switch combinations. When one record got a little too hard, I'd switch to another combination."

His potent little 283s wreaked havoc on the chassis of the big cars. Cal recalled his Impala hardtop saw three different frames under it, and the R/S 1966 Impala wagon

> **"I made my first run at the Nationals in 1969, and when I got back to my trailer, there were probably 25 guys there wanting to know who built my transmission."**
> **– Cal Method**

that followed in 1974–1975 saw four.

"The crossmember that the rear upper control arms bolted to would break and bust the frame. I finally added 12-inch by 12-inch triangular gussets on all four corners of the crossmember." The Methods kept three cars running from the mid-1970s into the 1980s. They hired Gary Roush to lend a hand in driving a bit in the late 1970s and early 1980s and later hired John McLaughlin.

When asked why Chevy, Cal responded that way back he had a worn-out 1952 Ford and was going to buy himself a Corvair. The salesman talked him out of the Corvair and into buying the Power Pack '57 wagon he had for sale. "Then I found out Chevys were cheaper than anything else to hop up." Though known for his prowess with the small-block, Cal and Mary Ann have run a few big-block combos. After winning the 1983 World Finals, Cal bought Joe Muller's A/SA, 427-powered Camaro. Cal's favorite combination? Their current 396-ci 375-hp Nova they started running back in 1993. Their line of 20 or so Chevys have brought them 10 division titles to date. At 74, Cal hopes there are more to come.

Jerry McClanahan

Jerry McClanahan was another standout who won big with a full-size Chevy wagon. His wins came in the form of NHRA World Championships in 1973, 1974, and 1978. The wagon was powered by a 283 that Jerry ran in both 2-barrel (195 hp) and 4-barrel (220 hp) configurations. The different combinations ran up to a dozen as Jerry ran the wagon at different times as an Impala, Bel Air, or Biscayne, all by simply changing the trim. As a six-passenger wagon by design, he could run even more classes by adding a third seat (nine-passenger). There was nothing overly trick about the winning wagon—just a strict attention to detail and plenty of trial and error. Jerry had 5 different sets of headers of different lengths and probably 20 different Quadrajet carbs. Behind the 283 ran a 2-speed Powerglide from a 6-cylinder car because it had a lower first gear.

Jerry built his own engines and relied upon Performance Machine in Azusa to do the machine work. As well as competing in class with the wagon, Jerry also ran brackets with it at his home track in Irwindale. He went the entire 1974 season without a loss, which enabled him to collect a bounty that the track and racers had offered up to anyone who could beat him. He took a few years off from racing before he returned in 1983 with a Super Street (10.90) 1965 Nova. He won four Division 7 championships; the last was in 1988 before he retired in 1989.

Cal and Mary Ann Method pose proudly with a sampling of the rewards earned over their six-plus decades of drag racing. True sportsmen, you couldn't meet a nicer couple. The Nova is still campaigned by the couple today. (Photo Courtesy Cal Method)

1988 before he retired in 1989.

What's not to like about a racer like Jerry McClanahan. Besides his three world titles, he was Division 7 champ four times, won six national events, and held class record multiple times. The wagon recorded a best of 13.60 at 99 mph. (Photo Courtesy Dave Kommel)

☆☆☆ THE BEST OF THE REST ☆☆☆

Looking back on the first 25 years of drag racing, Chevy was the established leader in nearly all door car categories—with the cars in Stock Eliminator at the forefront. Space limited the focus of this chapter to the more notable standouts, so here is a sampling of the best of the rest: a tip of the hat to the Chevys that made a difference, established trends, dominated class, and just plain dazzled us.

George Williams's Z/S 4-cylinder Vega panel was a 16-second terror. George knew how to set up a car. Would you believe this Vega could get air under those front wheels?! George played runner-up at the 1978 NHRA Winternationals, then won the Fallnationals in 1979, and the Gatornationals in 1980. (Photo Courtesy Dave Kommel)

☆☆☆ THE BEST OF THE REST ☆☆☆

Few sedan deliveries were as successful as John Archambault's Hydrophobia. Debuting late in 1966, "Archie" raced the delivery into 1970 and regularly ran well under L and H/SA class records. Initially powered by a 220-hp 283 and a Hydra-Matic transmission, John set NHRA and NASCAR records and in 1967 won the Super Stock Nationals. Running a 250-hp fuel-injected combo and Powerglide in 1970, the delivery recorded times of 13.56, nearly 4/10 of a second under the O/SA record. (Photo Courtesy Carl Rubrecht)

Back in 1966, Ernie Musser drove the competition bonkers when he ran a D/S record-setting 12.78 in his Honduras Red 1961 Corvette. The record, which stood for two years, was faster than Chryslers C/SA cars. The Corvette was sold at the end of 1966, and it went on to hold the class record into 1970 for Carmen Rotunda then Tony Festa. (Author's Collection)

Most competitors saw the Gunning brothers' laurel green wagon from this angle. The Gunnings debuted the wagon in 1966 and grabbed the H/S class at Springnationals. The wagon was a continuous class winner and record holder. (Photo Courtesy Ken Gunning)

There is an old saying, "So clean that you could eat off of it." Well, the term fits Jack and Ken Gunning's Jolly Green Giant perfectly. The attention to detail was second to none. This much-feared wagon looked as good as it ran and held class records multiple times. (Photo Courtesy Ken Gunning)

Tony Pizzi's much-feared 1968 Z28 Camaro set the F/S record at will and by late 1970 was capable of running 11.50-second times. On the national level, Tony took class at Indy in 1969 and the Winternationals in 1970. Tony drew the ire of competitors in September 1970 when he bombed the record, running an 11.68, which was quicker than even the C/S record of 11.69. (Photo Courtesy Carl Rubrecht)

☆ ☆ ☆ THE BEST OF THE REST ☆ ☆

Illinois resident Tom Akin's 1969 Chevy Kingswood wagon dominated AHRA action in 1969 and 1970, earning series championships both years. Powered by a 425-hp 427, the hefty 4,480-pound nine-passenger wagon recorded a best of 12.21 at 118 mph in 1971 and held multiple class records. (Photo Courtesy Ray Mann, www.quartermilestones.com Archive)

Bob Lambeck's meticulous 150-model '57 was a purpose-built D/Stocker that held class record in 1967 at 12.85 at 107.14 mph. The same year Bob won Division 7 points championship. A Joe Allread 0.058-over 283-hp 283 got the job done. (Author's Collection)

This M/S Cotton Candy '57 belonged to Larry Gibson of New Port Richey, Florida. Running on the 12.90 class record in 1970, the '57 is a prime example of the pride these Stock racers took in their cars. (Photo Courtesy Michael Mihalko)

Dave LeBrun won the 1971 Grandnationals in this B/S Camaro, defeating Joe DeLorenzo driving a LeBrun team car in the final. Bob Johnson bought the cars new from Scuncio Chevrolet in Rhode Island, where he worked as high-performance salesman/specialist. The Camaro, an original Z28, was upgraded to 427/425-hp status by Dave. He converted the car to SS/D for 1972 and sold it shortly after. An A/SA 1969 Camaro followed, which Dave used to win the Summernationals in 1974. (Author's Collection)

Another class champ from the Jim Waibel stable was this 270-hp J/Stocker. The True Grit name dates this one to 1969. Jim would ring high-12s out of the Bel Air, which was his last Chevy Junior Stocker. (Author's Collection)

Larry DeForrest warms the rubber on his 1965 Chevy II in preparation for yet another winning run. The Ramsey, Minnesota, resident was just one of many who saw success using the 250-hp 327 combo in S/S. (Photo Courtesy Gary Anderson)

Chapter Three

Super Stock's Finest

The NHRA debuted the Super Stock category in 1967 with 10 classes; SS/A through SS/E for stick cars, and SS/AA through SS/EA for automatics. By the end of the 1970s, the category had used up most of the alphabet and reached all the way to SS/X. The category classes, just like today, were based on vehicle weight divided by the NHRA-factored horsepower rating. As far back as the mid-1960s, the Big Three had been falsifying horsepower ratings to gain an advantage at the drag strip. With the countless number of combinations offered by Chevy, it should come as no surprise to anyone that they dominated the category.

Eddie Vasquez Sr.

Eddie Vasquez, a relative unknown from Elko, Nevada, and his red-on-red L79-powered Chevy II won the inaugural Super Stock Eliminator. Eddie flat-towed the SS/C car to the Winternationals and ran a 12.74 to defeat the SS/A 1965 Plymouth of Ed Miller in the final. Though relatively unknown, Eddie, a native of Southern California, was no greenhorn. He started racing in 1962 at Vacaville with a 1952 Chevy pickup. He graduated to a Chevy-powered B/Street Roadster before he and a buddy built a dirt-track car that they spent a year running at West Sacramento.

Early in 1964, greener pastures awaited in Elko, so Eddie loaded up the truck and hit the road. By this point, the truck was sporting twin 4-barrel carburetors on the 301 and with the addition of 5.13 gears behind the 4-speed it proved to be the fastest thing in the town. That is, until the fall of 1965 when a friend, Jack Skaggs, bought himself a 350-hp Chevy II. Eddie recalled, "We raced regularly. He'd win by 2 feet, then I'd win by 2

A 12.74 in the final round at the 1967 NHRA Winternationals earned Eddie and the L79 Deuce a trip to the winners circle. Part of the winnings included a gold-plated torque wrench, Valvoline sponsorship for a year, and Cragar wheels. (Photo Courtesy Eddie Vasquez)

feet." Tired of the seesaw battles, Eddie made a deal and purchased the Chevy II from Jack. They partnered briefly and they'd run the car at Salt Lake City or surrounding tracks every other week. They'd occasionally venture north to get out of the division and run in Seattle. Modifications to the 327 included a 0.030 overbore, Eddie's own fabricated headers, an Isky cam, and matched ports. Backing an owner-installed Muncie M-22 were 4.88 gears in the 12 bolt. Eddie shifted the Hurst at 6,500 rpm, but off the line he brought the mouse up to 2,500–3,000 rpm before he'd bury the throttle on the last yellow. Grabbing the track were Goodyear slicks that carried 8 pounds of pressure.

Eddie's first sighting on the national scene came at the 1965 NHRA World Finals, where the still-stock Chevy II did no better than the first alternate. Eddie made the show when a contestant fell out, but he immediately bowed out. Around this time, his partner, Skaggs, dropped from the scene and Butch Edison stepped in as helper.

At the 1967 Winternationals, Eddie won class with a 12.72 at 107.92 mph, which automatically became the class record that he had to run off of. If he was any quicker than 0.10 under, he'd automatically be disqualified. After winning the class on Saturday, the NHRA did the fuel check, pulled a head, weighed the car, approved it, and Eddie spent most of the night buttoning it back up in preparation for Sunday's eliminations. In the final against Miller, Eddie received the handicap start and had a good lead on Miller.

"I recall looking in my mirror. He was way back there, so I backpedaled. When I looked again, he was coming fast so I got back on it. He passed me in the lights and neither one of us knew who won. We had to wait for a call from the tower to find out."

Part of Eddie's winnings included $2,500 cash and an Isky cam and kit. Eddie recalled Ed Iskenderian talked him into running his engine on the Isky dyno. "They said they had never run a single 4-barrel 327 on their dyno. We arranged to bring the car back a couple months later. Out of the car and on the dyno, the 327 recorded 350 hp. They continued to play with different combinations, ending up

Eddie's luck ran short at the Springnationals in 1967 when he fell to the Comet wagon of Barrie Poole (seen here in the background). Note that Eddie's L79 Deuce was a rare non-SS model. (Author's Collection)

The L79-powered 1966 Chevy II was labeled the sleeper of the decade by many magazines. And it's no wonder, with its light weight and high horsepower the car was a major threat no matter where it ran. Tom Sappington and Frank Sanders running out of Scottsdale, Arizona, were the scourge of AHRA F-4 Super Stock, running 11.20 times with their Giant Killer. (Author's Collection)

with Grant pistons, Dykes rings, four different jets in the carb, and spark plugs of three different heat ranges. The final reading was 427 hp. A few more tweaks and just one more pull on the dyno, and they blew a rod out the side of the block. I had to be at Orange County for a program, so we hunted down a new 327 from a local Chevy dealer. We installed the engine but missed the date."

Eddie had B and T Automotive paint the car gold before the NHRA Springnationals. There Eddie lost in class to the Comet wagon of Barrie Poole. The Chevy II made a few more trips to Salt Lake City with a final trip to Seattle, where Eddie blew the engine. That was the end of his racing days.

"We hauled the car home and parked it beside the garage. I was married by this time and working on a family. A kid came by and bought the Chevy II. He put his own engine and transmission in it and roamed the streets before moving to Texas. The car met its demise when the kid wrapped it around a pole."

Bill "Grumpy" Jenkins

Bill Jenkins's 1966 Chevy II was capable of record-setting 11.11 times and was the odds-on favarite to win

the 1967 NHRA Winternationals. Hopes of victory were dashed early when the Grump drew a red light during class runoffs. It was one of Jenkins's last rides in the Chevy II; at Springnationals, he was behind the wheel of his first *Grumpy's Toy* Camaro. Two more Super Stock Camaros followed for the Grump, as well as a SS/D Nova, before he turned his attention to Pro Stock in 1970.

Grumpy Jenkins debuted this second Toy *in the fall of 1966 after losing his first Chevy II in a highway accident. The L79-powered* Toy *held the SS/C record with an 11.11 time. The car would reportedly hit top 10s while running B/FX in the early spring of 1967. (Author's Collection)*

Ed Hedrick installed a Turbo 400 behind his L72 (427–425 hp) to run SS/DA and cleaned house at the Gatornationals in 1970. His Camaro was the only Yenko car to win a major event. Ed is seen here at Englishtown running SS/E with a slick-shifted 4-speed. (Photo Courtesy Ed Hedrick)

As well as his own rides, which numbered up to three at a time, Jenkins prepared winners for a boatload of Stockers and Super Stock racers such as Dave Strickler, Dickie Ogles, and Ed Hedrick.

Jenkins was one of the few racers who had the ear of Chevrolet's Vince Piggins. Dating back to 1961 and his days with Dave Strickler, Jenkins was helped along with cars and parts from Chevrolet. Though limited by its own bureaucracy, Chevrolet protected its interests in drag racing. It was in no small part because of Jenkins close relationship with Piggins that the 375-hp Camaro was built specifically to do battle in the all-new Super Stock category.

Jenkins received his Ermine White Camaro in March, which was delivered by his right-hand man, Joe Tryson, who picked the car up at Chevy's Norwood assembly plant. The 375-hp engine was immediately refactored by the NHRA to 425, which placed the car in SS/C. That was rightly so because it was the same engine rated at 425 hp in the limited 1965 SS396 Chevelle and the 1965 Corvette.

In preparing the Camaro, Jenkins's 396 went through the usual balance and blueprint. Carbs were Jenkins's specialty, and the 785 Holley was modified, as was the

factory aluminum intake it was perched upon. A number of camshafts were trialed with Jenkins usually settling on either a General Kinetics or Sig Erson bump stick. Factory forged pistons were used to squeeze out 12.5:1 compression. A slick-shifted Muncie transmission stuffed with BorgWarner gears with a 2.36 first backed the engine,

In SS/C class competition, Jenkins's Camaro ran times in the 11.10s. That was not bad for a 396 factored by the NHRA to 425 hp. Ed Terry, behind the wheel of Huston Platt's 427 Fairlane, no doubt felt the sting of the 425 hp. (Author's Collection)

and 4.88 gears usually filled the 12-bolt rear end. To help get the weight on the right end of the car, many front-end parts were acid dipped, including the hood, fenders, and front crossmember.

At the Camaro's Springnationals debut, Jenkins handily won the class with an 11.77 but fell in elimination to Chrysler team player Ronnie Sox. After losing to Jere Stahl's street hemi at the NHRA Nationals in 1966, Jenkins returned in 1967 to seek revenge. It wasn't easy because both Chrysler and Ford had all their team players out in force: Sox & Martin arrived with three cars; Bob Brown was in his SS/A record-holding 1965 Plymouth; Arlen Vanke; Ron Mancini; Don Grotheer; and Jere Stahl hoped for a repeat win. Ford pinned its hopes on the 427-powered Fairlane and drivers Ed Terry, Don Nicholson, Hubert Platt, and Jerry Harvey.

As eliminations proceeded, the Fords and Chryslers took care of each other, and all the Fords were done by the third round. Jenkins advanced and drove his way to the final round with times as quick as 11.45. In the final, he faced Bob Brown and his much-quicker Plym-outh. Allowing for a handicap start, Jenkins got the lead on Brown, never looked back, and took the win with an 11.55 at 115.97 mph to a losing 11.10 at 125.52.

Though Jenkins didn't win another national event until 1970, his cars wreaked havoc at the 1968 NHRA World Finals in Tulsa. Ed Hedrick drove Jenkins's 1967 Camaro, now with A/MP to a final-round appearance in Modified Eliminator; and in Super Stock, Jenkins drove his 375-hp SS/D Nova to the finals where he faced Strickler's Z28 Camaro. It was a win-win situation for Jenkins because he had prepared the world-champ Camaro for Strickler. Those 302s were screamers and this one produced an estimated 450 hp. Helping to produce its final run 11.80 ET was a 0.030 bore increase, an M-22 transmission, and 5.38 rear gears.

The Rat Pack

The *rat* motor more than held its own in the world of Super Stock thanks to the efforts of guys like Jenkins and Detroit's famed Rat Pack. The loosely formed pack consisted of Dick Arons, Wally Booth, Odus Rigsby,

A highlight of Dave Strickler's illustrious drag racing career was his Super Stock World Championship win in 1968. In the final, Dave defeated the SS/D Nova of Grumpy Jenkins with an 11.80. The Camaro's drivetrain consisted of a 0.030-over Jenkins-built 302 that produced a reported 450 hp. (Photo Courtesy Michael Pottie)

Gordy Foust, and Lance Hill. All of them ran big-block-powered cars. Arons was the pack's only Detroit native, and Odus, Wally, and Gordy were all from Appalachia (Tennessee and West Virginia) and came north for work in the auto industry.

The Rat Pack title was coined by *National Dragster* in early 1968 when it reported race results. The pack began around 1966 when Booth, who ran his Chevelle at Detroit, had issues with the car and approached the younger Dick Arons for help. Dick, who had been running rough shod through the ranks with his own car, cured Booth's ills, and the friendship solidified. A tight bunch, the pack of five raced together, pitted together, wrenched on their cars together, and hung around together.

Lance Hill said, "Being a member was limited only to the initial bunch. Even Dick 'Big M' Maskin and Mike Fons, who raced a lot with us and lived in Detroit, weren't in." Mike, in his A/MP 1967 Camaro, became Street Eliminator World Champion in 1969 with one of Dick Arons's motors. Lance said, "Dickie was a sharp-thinking engine and driveline guy—largely self-taught. He initially worked in the back machine shop of Midwest Auto Parts in Berkeley. He soon made some sort of deal wherein he used the name Dick Arons Racing Engines. Dickie built a brand-new 325-hp 396 Camaro to race in 1968 and surprised the hell out of me by saying he would rather watch and learn from the car going down the drag strip than by driving, and the guys suggested

Wally Booth ran this 375-hp 396-ci Chevelle in B/S during 1966 and stepped up to SS/D in 1967 with the addition of an aftermarket intake and cam. Wally won class at every national event entered in 1967. (Photo Courtesy Michael Pottie)

me to drive. I bought in and drove all year; ran the same car in 1968 repainted maroon when Dickie decided we would all go maroon with gold leaf lettering.

"Typically, Wally went his own way and left his car green. It was a pretty car too. By 1970, we were back to banging heads in the first year of Pro Stock and pretty much going our own ways. Things were never the same."

For their efforts, the pack won the Division 3 crown in 1968 (Booth-S/S), took class at numerous national events, and set their share of class records.

Running SS/GA with a 325-hp 396, Dick Arons and his 1967 Camaro played runner-up at the 1969 World Finals. The 325-hp engine/Camaro combo was one of the winningest in S/S history. (Photo Courtesy Bob Thanish/Dale Schafer Collection)

Truppi and Kling

The tri-state area of New York, New Jersey, and Connecticut produced its share of winners with a good many coming from the New Jersey shop of Ralph Truppi and Tommy Kling. The pair's success dates back to the mid-1960s when they first opened shop in Green Brook. One of their many customers was a gentleman named Ray Allen, whose Corvette, with the help of a Ralph Truppi–built 283, was hammering them in the Sport Production category. When T-K decided to get serious about drag racing with an injected '57 Chevy wagon in 1967, they called on Ray to man the controls. The *Terrible Tangerine* wagon was one slick piece: a K/S record holder capable of running 4/10 under the class record. The legend of Truppi-Kling took root, and through 1971, the outfit was responsible for a reported 80 class records.

T-K made the move to Super Stock in 1970, and after turning down a factory deal from Chrysler, built an LS6-powered Chevelle ragtop. The story goes that Tommy Kling was initially after an LS6-powered Corvette, but Chevrolet couldn't get him one. Looking at their options, they settled on the Chevelle. The car fit perfectly on the SS/EA class break, a class that up to that point was dominated by Mopars. Many felt T-K didn't stand a chance.

Working out a deal with Briggs Chevrolet, T-K took delivery of the Chevelle in May, and with just 61 miles showing on the odometer, they tore into the car. With only weeks until its planned debut, there wasn't a lot of time to go through the car. Starting with the 454, Tony Feil was called on to perform much of the machine work while Ralph prepared the parts that would fill the mill: 0.030-over TRW pistons (with 0.120 off the top and 0.120 off the block), a factory aluminum hi-rise intake that mounted an 800 Holley, factory rods, crank, and a Sig Erson cam to actuate the 2.19 intake and 1.84 exhaust valves. A small-block dual-point distributor sparked the Champions while spent gases exited through Hooker headers. Power was transmitted through a Vitar-prepped Turbo 400 to a 5.14-equipped rear end.

Debuting at the 1970 NHRA Summernationals, Allen drove the car through 1971. Outside of the initial outing, he won class at every national event he entered. The car put the team of Truppi-Kling and Allen in the national spotlight after winning the World Finals and Supernationals in 1970. Although the team failed to win its first national event, it seems it put enough fear into the Chrysler camp that the manufacturer built a ringer in an attempt to sideline the Chevelle.

The ringer came in the form of Jack Werst's *Mr. 5 and 50* Plymouth Super Bird. The car had quite a few not-so-legal modifications that even if it did win, it would fail inspection. To begin with, the Hemi measured out to 512 inches and was said to be capable of times in the 10.40s. The Superbird and Chevelle came face to face at Indy in 1970, and Allen was handed the win after Werst drew a red light. Allen took class with an 11.37 over Bob Lambeck, who fouled with an 11.42. Capable of 11-flat times, Allen took the 11.55 class record from Lambeck in November with an 11.33 at 125.96 mph. When the Briggs sponsorship ended at the close of the 1971 season, Truppi-Kling purchased the Chevelle and 1970 C30

In 1970, Truppi-Kling walked into Mopar's stomping ground of SS/EA and trounced it with their LS6 Chevelle. These guys could build winners. Over the years, they were responsible for something like 80 class record holders. Almost all were Chevys. (Photo Courtesy Michael Pottie)

Ray Allen, seen here at Island Dragway, replaced Bill Fusco behind the wheel of Truppi-Kling's Terrible Tangerine *in 1968. Few knew how to build horsepower like Ralph and Tommy. By the end of 1969, their injected wagon was capable of 12.70 times on a 13.14 J/S class record. (Photo Courtesy Tom Ronca)*

Six-cylinder springs from a 1965 Chevelle, loose bushings, and Koni shocks gave the Chevelle its lift. In this instance, so did a trusty floor jack. Four-inch Cragars mount Moroso tires. Rear tires are 12-inch M&Hs. (Photo Courtesy Tommy Ronca)

Ray Allen and the Chevelle grabbed the SS/EA record at the 1970 season to end Supernationals with an 11.33. When Ray moved to Pro Stock in 1972, Claude Urevig bought the Chevelle and raced it through 1974 to set the SS/DA record in July that year with a 10.78 at 128.20. Tom Camperlengo was the next owner who ran the car. It wore the 1971 trim well into the 1980s. (Photo Courtesy Michael Pottie)

hauler from them for a paltry $1,500. Claude Urevig, a part of the more-than-capable T-K Performance team, bought the Chevelle when Allen moved up to Pro Stock in 1972. Claude continued the winning ways and took class honors and set class records over the next few seasons. The Chevelle was then sold to Tom Camperlengo, who ran the car into the 1980s. When Tom passed away

in 1989, his widow sold the car to Ray Allen. Ray initiated a restoration of the car before Chip Gerst purchased it from him and finished the job.

Bernie Agaman

Bernie Agaman was another unforgettable Truppi-Kling graduate. Bernie started racing back in 1964 behind

At the World Finals in 1975, Bernie Agaman polished off Jeff Velde and his Bob Glidden Race Cars Mustang before facing Paul Rossi's Hemi Barracuda in the final. There, Bernie defeated the Barracuda with a resounding 10.29 at 130.24 mph. (Photo Courtesy Dave Kommel)

the wheel of a brand-new Mustang, a car he flat-towed home from the dealership and immediately dug into. He recalled having to explain to his mom what those brackets (used for towing) were sticking out of the front of his new car. He ran the Mustang for a few years in F/SA before moving on to a few different Fairlanes. He raced Fords sparingly through 1970 as he focused on operating his first service station. He eventually owned three stations and ran a booming U-Haul business.

A 1968 Nova was built to run H/SA through 1972 that helped earn Bernie the Division 1 Super Stock crown. When asked why he switched to Chevy, Bernie flat-out replied, "I got tired of losing." He swapped the drivetrain from the Nova into a 1968 Camaro to run SS/LA, and on its first day out, the car ran an 11.70, an astounding 0.4 seconds under the existing class record. The following week, he took class at Indy over the 1965 Chevy of Willard Wright.

A just-as-competitive SS/D Camaro came next before Bernie debuted the renowned *Bayonne Missile*: a low compression, 454-powered 1971 Corvette. Factory rated at 425 hp, the NHRA was quick to refactor the mill to 435. A Holley 780 sat atop an Edelbrock Tarantula intake with further support from Cam Dynamics and Moroso. The motor was backed by a Vitar-prepped Turbo 400.

The Corvette debuted at the 1974 NHRA Gatornationals and fell squarely into the SS/DA, a class wrought with mighty Mopars. Bernie set the class record in May with a 10.78 at 128.20 mph and held it for most of the year. Running 100 pounds heavy, the Corvette cranked a best of 10.58 at 129.12 mph in 1974. Bernie spent approximately $15,000 to build the car, and that included the purchase price. He probably spent another

$5,000 to eliminate breakage issues, which pretty much were all related to the independent rear suspension (IRS). When he built the car, Bernie went with a live Dana rear with the understanding it would be legal. Uh, nope. The NHRA clarified the rule and stated they'd only accept a Dana center section. The independent Corvette suspension had to be retained.

With the help of SRD (speed research development) Race Cars, a bulletproof IRS was built over the winter of 1974–1975 that used the Dana 60 center section, fabricated trailing arms, and half shafts that carried Chevy C60 truck U-joints. The Dana was filled with 5.13 gears.

Refactored to SS/CA in 1975, the Corvette dominated the class and won four out of five division races. Bernie played runner-up at the Gatornationals before he won the Summernationals, Grandnationals, and World Finals. He qualified number one at the finals, ahead of the Pontiac wagon of Jack Mullins and the heavy-hitting Mopars of Dave Boertman, Ted Flack, Dave Wren, Ed Hamburger, and Judy Lilly. In the final round, he defeated the Mopar of Paul Rossi with a 10.29 at 130.24 mph to earn his only World Championship title.

It was an unbelievable year for Bernie, who compiled more WCS points than any other sportsman racer and was voted Sportsman driver of the year by his peers. In September, Bernie reset his own class record with a 10.21 at 132.15 mph at Atco. The record was held until the NHRA erased it in April 1978.

Bernie took a break in action before he returned in 1978 to run an SRD Pro Stock Monza. He partnered with Ray Locke and ran the small-inch big-block car through 1979 before he retired.

The NHRA factored Bernie Agaman's combo for 1975 and moved it into SS/CA. The blistered hood, though not available in 1971, was an NHRA legal replacement. It sure helped get air to the Holley carburetor. The first time out in the Corvette, Bernie ran a 10.72 on an 11.15 SS/DA class record. Agaman admitted there was plenty of breakage the first year out with the Corvette. "I might have pocketed $200." (Author's Collection)

Bernie walked into Chrysler's stomping ground of SS/DA with his 1971 Corvette and sent them packing. At Indy in 1974, Bernie won class with a 10.80 to defeat the Hemi 'Cuda of Roger Englund. At the time, the Corvette was the class record holder with a 10.78 at 128.20 mph. (Photo Courtesy Bob Martin)

> **We really felt [like] they were out to get us. After all, they had backing from the manufacturers who wanted their new cars to win."**
> **– Terry Hardy**

The Hardy Boys

Leading the Tri-Five charge in the world of Super Stock was Southern California's Pat and Terry Hardy, aka the Hardy Boys. The brothers first became involved in drag racing back around 1966 when they took Terry's '55 out to Fontana to bracket race. The mechanics were left up to Pat, who proved more than capable over the years thanks to the mentoring of guys such as Joe Allread and Gene Ohly. Pat spent a number of years working for Gene at the famed Evan's Speed Equipment in El Monte. Pat was like a sponge and absorbed everything.

Meanwhile, Terry went to work for Hooker Headers, which used his '55 to design the Tri-Five fenderwell headers that became so popular.

The brothers got serious about drag racing in 1972 with an SS/V '55 wagon and set both ends of the class record in June at Sacramento when they recorded a 13.86 at 99.34 mph. On their return trip home to Orange, they rolled the ramp truck just outside of Bakersfield. The incident put Pat in the hospital for a week with some serious injuries, and it pretty much destroyed the wagon. The brothers were given a decent replacement wagon by a man who saw their story in *National Dragster*, and within a few weeks they were back in action. Pat said, "We had a pretty good fixture in the garage with a hoist on it where we could switch bodies. We would do this with different cars to run different classes. It would take about half a day to complete."

The year 1973 saw the Hardys switch from the wagon to this Bel Air and from an auto transmission to stick. Leaf springs and ladder bars made for a nice launch. This SS/T Bel Air was good for record 12.50 times. Over their career, the Hardys set or reset in the neighborhood of 90 class records. (Photo Courtesy Pat Hardy)

The Hardy brothers' first serious effort began with this SS/V wagon in 1972. Captured here at Irwindale, the model 210 wagon survived long enough to set both ends of the class record. (Photo Courtesy Terry Hardy)

The brothers moved away from the automatic transmission in 1973 and never looked back. Terry said, "It was a lot more fun to bang gears than drive a Powerglide." Pat built the ladder bar suspension, and the car broke a lot of parts because it hooked so hard. "We actually broke the mainshaft in half using a BorgWarner T-16 at Bakersfield one year." (Photo Courtesy Terry Hardy)

A '55 hardtop followed the wagon late in 1973 that the Hardy Boys ran through 1974. With the switch to the new car, the brothers also made the move from a Powerglide transmission to a stick. Super Stock rules of the day limited transmission choices to what was available the year the car was produced. The only stick option in 1955 was the 3-speed, and the brothers chose the BorgWarner T-16. This was the strongest 3-speed available from Chevy and was used behind big-block-powered Camaros and Chevelles during the late 1960s.

Put behind the potent 265, the brothers went through a lot of parts. Pat said, "BorgWarner had a parts warehouse just outside of Pico Rivera, and we used up just about everything they had. We'd buzz the engine to 8,800 rpm coming off the line and shift at the same RPM." Driveshafts and rear ends were also a problem. "We couldn't keep driveshafts or rear ends in it. We finally went to a custom-made chrome-moly driveshaft and a Dana 60 with a Summers Brothers spool. We had Schiefer nickel and steel ring-and-pinion gears and we'd only be getting about 10 to 12 rounds out of them. We finally figured out why after breaking off the left wheel on one run. Summers had cut the left axle too long, and when we installed it and tightened it down, it would push the ring gear away from the pinion, changing the backlash."

The brothers debuted the easily recognizable blue and white '55 business coupe late in 1974 and ran it through 1975. The car received its share of ink, and its performance helped establish the Hardys nationally. The brothers racked up wins and the NHRA rewarded them by factoring their combination.

"We really felt [like] they were out to get us. After all, they had backing from the manufacturers who wanted their new cars to win." Terry recalled winning class at the 1975 Winternationals and being disqualified. "We had to tear down, which was fine, but then they told us they wanted to look at a connecting rod. We were running stock rods, and you couldn't do much with them beyond bush the small end to make the deck height right. They accused us of running rods that were longer than stock. Joe Allread was there backing us up, saying everyone was bushing the rods to make the deck height right. The NHRA still didn't buy it. But two weeks later they changed the rules."

The brothers' '56 business coupe that followed was pretty much the accumulation of all they had learned up to that point. Running SS/N, O, and P at different times, the '56 was what Pat referred to as "almost a Pro Stock '56."

Propelling the 3,300 pounder to new records was a 0.058-over 265-ci engine. The heart of any good engine is the camshaft, and since he developed a great relationship with Chase Knight at Crane Cams, Pat had the cams ground to his desired specs. Crane valve springs (which could last as little as a day) and 1.6:1 intake and 1.5:1 exhaust rockers filled out the valvetrain.

Although in color images the paint looked black and white, it was actually white and Ford-truck blue. The brothers won the Division 7 Super Stock title in 1976 and 1978. (Photo Courtesy Terry Hardy)

Terry Hardy recalled standing the '56 up on the back bumper at Bowling Green Raceway during the Sportsnationals. "Those Eastern boys had seen the car in National Dragster *but were skeptical. However, when they saw that, they knew it was the real deal. Until the 50/50 weight rule, the car would hook up in water." (Photo Courtesy Terry Hardy)*

Though modifications to the heads were limited by the rules, they spent a lot of time on the ports, tweaking the exhaust side. To cover up the not-so-legal mods, they glass-beaded and shot-peened the surface to bring back the stock appearance. When it came to induction, the brothers had three variances of the Edelbrock Pro Ram manifold to choose from. Each featured a modified plenum and runners that were reworked to match the ports. Pat was quick to mention the helping hand provided by Jim McFarland at Edelbrock.

Perched atop the manifold were twin Carter WCFB carbs. The brothers' connections at Carter paid off in spades as the manufacturer supplied countless parts. Mods to the carbs included taking care of the vacuum-operated secondary flap valves. The engine had to reach a certain RPM or vacuum for the flaps to open, so Pat fabricated tiny Allen set screws that held them open. The screws were hidden behind the linkage, so tech inspectors never saw the modification.

Filling the cylinders were nice, light Venolia pistons that were worked over by Larry Tores, who added gas ports and hand-lapped the rings to fit the pistons. The factory compression ratio was pretty much maintained at 9 to 1. However, Pat ran the minimum 0.018-inch deck height and thin 0.021-inch head gaskets. The piston pins were made of light H-11 tool steel and actually flexed, which left cylinder head marks on the quench/flat side of the piston dome. Hooker 1¾-inch fenderwell headers expelled the spent fuel.

The 3-speed transmission the brothers had been running was replaced with a Doug Nash 4+1 modified to run three gears. The first gear ratio was a 2.98; second, 1.77; and third, 1.07. As Terry recalled, the one-two shift came a second after leaving the line, and he was in third gear

The inside of the Hardys' '56 was all business and featured a Moroso cable-drive tach, Autometer gauges, Hurst shifter, and line lock. A six-point cage protected Terry in case things went awry. (Photo Courtesy Terry Hardy)

halfway down the track. A 30-pound flywheel helped get the car moving, and at higher-elevation tracks they ran a 17-pound flywheel and wide-ratio gears. Inside the Dana 60 were 6.50 gears that made the Chevy trip the lights at 8,600 rpm.

Rear-end hop was controlled by modified leaf springs and 36-inch ladder bars that were fabricated by Pat. Regarding the front suspension, the factory rubber A-arm bushings were replaced with solid bushings that were oxidized black to look like original rubber parts. To place greater weight on the rear of the car, the brothers had the front body panels acid dipped and hid the weight out back. A lead tray was cut into the top of the fuel tank, and a lead-filled crossmember was added to mount the shocks. The boys went as far as to fill the taillights with lead, noting that they didn't work anyway.

The Hardys retired in 1982, having grown tired of break-out rules and index racing. Terry summed it up by saying, "Racing is supposed to be about going fast. Our final race was at Sacramento. We lost to a used-car-lot Chevelle that was four classes below us."

The WCFB carbs wouldn't clear the hood, so the Hardys jacked around with the motor mounts and tweaked the hood. The quickest time for the '56 was an 11.44 at 114.91 mph recorded at Fremont. (Photo Courtesy Terry Hardy)

Terry Hardy heats the 13x30 Goodyears prior to what was no doubt another great run. Pressure in the slicks ran around 4 to 5 pounds. Aluminum Cragar Super Trick wheels dropped unsprung weight. (Photo Courtesy Pat Hardy)

Bill Hanes—S/S World Champ

Hailing from Lansing, Michigan, Bill Hanes attended his first NHRA Nationals in 1959 at the age of 16 with a dragster he built at home in his parents' garage. In 1962, he switched to running Stock and joined the famed Chevair Racing Team with a 327-powered 1962 Bel Air. He had his first taste of national event victory when he won G/SA at the 1964 Nationals with the car. Bill debuted his 350-powered 1968 Impala in 1970, which was the car he won the NHRA Super Stock World Championship with in 1973. The Impala was rebodied before the 1975 season as a 1968 Biscayne, and it racked up wins and records through 1981. Bill switched to running Super Gas, and with a 454-ci small-block for power, the Biscayne recorded times in the 9.50s.

Bill Hanes's World Championship-winning 1969 Impala is seen here in 1974 at the Popular Hot Rodding magazine meet held at Martin US-131 Dragway. Bill defeated the Chevelle of Roger Rosebush in the Super Stock final. Record times of 12.30s at 109 were the norm for the small-block Chevy. (Photo Courtesy Bruce Nelson)

Bobby Warren

Another graduate of the Tri-Five Junior Stock days was Bobby Warren of Clinton, North Carolina. Bobby was a second-generation tobacco farmer who made a living by working the fields but got his kicks on the quarter mile. Bobby was involved in organized drag racing since the early 1950s, and made his first pass at Sanford, North Carolina, in his 1953 Chevy. A number of Chevys followed before Bobby got serious in 1965 with a 270-hp '57 model 210. He teamed up with his brother-in-law, Hayward Register, and through 1968 they compiled numerous class wins and national records. Like many winning Stock class racers at the time, Bobby insisted there was nothing secretive about his combination and stated a good blueprint and a strict attention to detail was the difference between winning and losing.

A few Camaro Stockers followed before Bobby finally got serious about chasing Division 2 points. His efforts culminated with a World Championship in 1970 with his J/S Nova. Two more championship crowns followed in 1974 and 1978 with a pair of Super Stock Camaros. At his first World Finals, Bobby's 255-hp 350 Nova defeated the Dodge wagon of Bob Burkitt in the finals with a 12.21.

Bobby recalled going through a lot of cars, as people would offer to buy them and he wasn't the type to grow attached to one. The Nova was sold to 1967 World Champion George Cureton immediately after the World Finals and in its place came a K/S 1969 Chevelle. Though Bobby said the Chevelle wasn't a great car when compared to the Nova because "the rear suspension was wrong," he found the LM1 that powered the car to his liking. He proceeded to win the Springnationals in 1971 and defeated the J/SA Charger of Dave Boertman. The 255-hp engine didn't need a lot of "breathing on" initially as it was an underrated powerplant to start with.

"It wasn't until more people started running them that we had to start working on them." ForgedTrue pistons filled the cylinders and a Lunati cam worked the valves.

A wet weekend at the 1974 Sportsnationals didn't deter Bobby Warren from winning the event. He defeated the Barracuda of Terry Earwood in the final. Additional wins at the Springnationals and World Finals earned Bobby his second of three World Championships (he also won in 1970 and 1978). (Photo Courtesy Michael Cochran)

Bobby wrapped up the year by being crowned the NHRA Division 2 points champion. Chrysler came rapping on the door, hoping to persuade him to jump ship, but true to Chevy, he passed on the factory offer. In 1972, Bobby made the switch to Super Stock and carried on his winning ways to take both the Gatornationals and Springnationals with the Chevelle.

Although he attended Nashville's Auto and Diesel College for one year in his youth, Bobby's talents came naturally. He said, "Taking an interest and wanting to do it was the drive for me." Not one to rely on the trick-of-the-week parts, Bobby used his own means to stay one step ahead of the competition. Though a lightening of body parts was generally frowned upon by the sanc-

tioning bodies, the Super Stock Camaros that Bobby campaigned through the mid-1970s had body panels washed in his homemade vat of *cleaning agents*. Fenders, doors, hoods, and bumpers were all washed to remove excess weight.

Bobby's desire to succeed culminated in a total of 15 national event wins. By far, his most successful year was 1978, when he won four national events and his third World Championship along with pocketing a cool $15,000 for winning NHRA's Grace Cup. His last big win was in 2004 at Bristol behind the wheel of his Chevy-powered Super Stock Firebird. In winning Bristol, the 69-year-old became the oldest person to ever win a national event.

The final round at the 1978 NHRA World Finals saw Bobby Warren (in the far lane) defeat Jim Weakland on the brakes. Bobby's four national event wins that year earned him his third world title. (Author's Collection)

Larry Tores

On the West Coast, Larry Tores came into his own when Bobby was in the midst of his championship years. Larry grew up in Southern California during the early 1960s, back when drag strips littered the landscape and a favorite pastime was cruising the boulevard. A little stoplight action was always in the cards, and Larry did his share in a 348-powered 1958 Chevy. As a teenager, life couldn't get any better. He traded in the Chevy for a 425A 1960 Pontiac and ran the car through the end of the decade, winning more than his share of trophies and stoplight jaunts. He earned his first class record behind the wheel of an injected Corvette that he ran in 1971 and 1972. In 1973, he took the wheel of a SS/MA Chevy II wagon owned by Larry Edelbrock. Tores built the 250-hp 327 for the car that won a couple point meets and, for a time, held the class record with a 12.04 113.79 mph.

Larry partnered with Gary Bosz in 1974 and the pair debuted an evolutionary SS/HA 1967 Chevy II. Powered by a 275-hp 327 and backed by a Powerglide transmission, the car featured a full roll cage and four-link rear suspension. Both items at the time weren't standard Super Stock fare. As Larry recalled, "Knowing the issues these unibody Chevy IIs had with chassis flex, and an unwillingness to go down the track straight, I knew we had to do something a little more sophisticated than what was considered the norm at the time."

The Chevy II was a junkyard rescue that was built in Larry's home garage. For those who enjoyed reading *Popular Hot Rodding* back then, the build was chronicled through a few issues of the magazine. Initial plans called for a ladder bar rear suspension, but after conferring with chassis builder Ron Butler, a four-link was incorporated instead. Before the suspension went in, the rear frame rails were relocated for tire clearance. Being the budget build it was, Tores and Bosz went about the task themselves in Larry's single-car garage. They modified drill bits so they could drill out the factory spot welds. It was just a matter of plugging in the electric drill and hitting the factory welds. Gary attacked one rail while Larry did the other. When the drills got too hot to hold, they'd set them aside, pick up another, and carry on. When done, they had moved the rails in 2¾ inches per side. Although they ran 11.5 tires, the relocated rails and Gary's fabricated wheel tubs allowed for up to 14 inches of tire. The Chevy II is said to be the first (possibly the second) four-

You would be hard pressed to name a better small-block than the 327. Larry Tores used the oh-so-popular 250-hp version in the Tores & Edelbrock wagon to set the SS/MA record with a 12.04 at 113.79 mph. (Photo Courtesy Dave Kommel)

link Super Stock car built. Larry recalled that the four-link really planted the car and didn't do time-wasting big wheelstands.

Before the car was completed, the NHRA factored the 327 to 285 hp, which moved it from pretty well bang-on the class break to approximately 90 pounds over. It didn't make much difference to this combo. The pair debuted the car at the 1975 NHRA Winternationals, where they ran an 11.30 to take class over the 'Cuda of Ron Debler.

Larry built the 327 that was backed by a Marv Ripes A-1 Powerglide. The Powerglide initially ran the factory 1.82 low gear before they made a switch to a 1.98 first. The change helped set the class record in July at Fremont, where the Chevy II recorded an 11.10 at 121.62 mph. Larry told Marv that he thought the car could run a 10-second time at Sacramento, a known *fast track*. Up until then, no Powerglide car had ever run in the 10s. According to Larry, Marv said, "Well, maybe you're ready for the 10s, but I don't think the car is."

Larry headed to Sacramento for the next WCS points meet, where he dropped the SS/HA record with an 11.06. The following evening, the car ran a pair of 11.06s, an 11.03, and 11 seconds flat. No doubt the Chevy was loving the cool night air. Not ready for the 10s you say? In the final round of eliminations, Larry faced the Chevy of Mike McGraf and beat him with a 10.94. The barrier was broken, and by the end of the season, the Chevy II was knocking out 10s everywhere. Tores and Bosz closed the season and won three of the four Division 7 points meets and was runner-up at the fourth. They won the division title 1,000 points ahead of second-place finisher.

When the pair set out to build the car, they agreed to run it for one year then sell it. After the 1975 World Finals, Gary placed an ad in *Nationals Dragster* and offered the car for sale at a firm $10,000. There were few tire kickers but nothing serious until John Lingenfelter called to say he wanted the car. With plans to run the Winternationals, Gary told him he could have the car after the race. A stipulation was that he and Larry would keep any winnings. After they won the class with a 10.87, Larry battled his way to the final where he faced the Graf Enterprises SS/MA Corvette driven by Lingenfelter. Larry took the win with a 10.83 and the $10,000 that came with it. After Larry treated everyone to dinner, John paid up the

Larry transitioned from Stock to Super Stock in 1972 with this fuel-injected 1960 Corvette. Capable of 12.20s, the Corvette was Larry's first record holder. (Photo Courtesy Dave Kommel)

A 275-hp 327 backed by a Powerglide capable of 10-second times? Who would have ever thought! Larry thanks Marv Ripes at A-1 for helping make it happen. Larry has always had a great relationship with Marv and built parts for him after he went into business for himself (T&D Machine Products) in 1975. (Photo Courtesy Dave Kommel)

$10,000 for the car in crisp $100 bills. Lingenfelter ran the Chevy II for a year and opened the season with a win in the IHRA's first Super Modified eliminator.

Toward the end of 1977, Larry went to work building a C/Econo Altered Opel. The car went together with a 100-inch wheelbase, Mark Williams chassis kit, Fiberglass Trends body, and 292-ci Chevy, which came courtesy of *Car Craft* magazine's Rick Voegelin. Sherm Gunn of M&S Race Cars mounted the body after he stretched it 4 inches. For class, the car needed to weigh 2,250 pounds, but it fell short of the mark by something like 650 pounds, which required the guys to add weight here, there, and everywhere on the car.

A 317-ci engine was put together for the car (3.25 stroke) that helped Larry play runner-up in the division in 1978 and win it in 1979. The Opel held the class record through most of 1979 with a 9.48 at 141.50 mph. When it came to national events, Larry had three runner-

A Ron Butler–designed four-link rear suspension saw the Chevy II hook and go, minus the time-consuming wheelstands we all love to see. The sticker on the rear bumper advertises the short-lived California Super Stock Association. About a dozen cars were involved, and it lasted maybe six months. (Photo Courtesy Dave Kommel)

up finishes with the car before he won the 1980 NHRA Winternationals. "Comp was a fun place to race. In 1975, in Super Stock you could run as hard as you could. There was no break out. In 1976, they stayed no break out at national events, but the WCS races had a break out. So, a lot of guys switched from Super Stock to Comp." Larry ran Comp for a few seasons before he took a break. He returned a few years later with an Econo Altered Buick.

"Jim McFarland called and asked if I'd be interested in running a Buick. I got together with John Bally from *Hot Rod* magazine, who was writing tech articles for Buick. Buick had the Stage II V-6 program, aiming for Indy, and John thought there was room in the budget for a drag car." John asked Larry to put together a proposal for Herb Fishel, head of Buick's Special Products Group. It was around that time in 1982 when General Motors started getting back into racing (drag racing, IROC, Indy, et al.). The floodgates were open,

> **"Comp was a fun place to race. In 1975, in Super Stock you could run as hard as you could. There was no break out. In 1976, they stayed no break out at national events, but the WCS races had a break out. So, a lot of guys switched from Super Stock to Comp."**
>
> **– Larry Tores**

and through 1983 into 1984, Larry received quite a bit of factory support. He ran a Century, then a Somerset body using the same chassis, and won three national events before he retired. He remained connected with Buick's Special Products Group and did research and development through 1988.

When the NHRA debuted C/Econo Altered in 1978, Larry Tores partnered with Jim Shenberg and jumped in with this fiberglass Opel. A single 4-barrel small-block Chevy nestled between a Mark Williams chassis saw the car dominate the class with record mid-9-second times. (Photo Courtesy Dave Kommel)

Lingenfelter's Racing Roots

John Lingenfelter raced everything from Stock to Pro Stock, from Chevys to Oldsmobiles, and quite possibly everything in between. He first gained national prominence in 1972 when he debuted an SS/NA, 255-hp 1969 Camaro and won the U.S. Nationals. He tried his hand in Pro Stock with Bob Glidden's old Pinto in 1974 before he returned to the Chevy camp with a 1973 Corvette. With its 0.060-overbore 195-hp 350, the Elkhart green machine was the scourge of SS/MA in 1975. It won the Winternationals and took class at the Gators and Indy and turned 11.30 times.

The Corvette was sold to Charlie Graf, although John continued to drive it through 1976. Things went sideways in 1977 as John purchased Bob Glidden's failed Pro Stock Monza and—horror of all horrors—ran it in Econo Altered with a Cleveland Ford for power. He returned to his senses in 1976 when he purchased Larry Tores's Chevy II and won almost everything in sight.

John continued racing into the 2000s and ran Comp and Pro Stock Truck. He also spent time on the salt flats, where he hit 298 mph in a Chevy-powered Firebird. Business was booming at Lingenfelter Performance Engineering. When it came to Chevy performance, John was the go-to guy. He gained a favorable reputation with Chevy and was hired to perform research and development work for the manufacturer.

When John was at his peak, he crashed his Sport Compact Cavalier at the NHRA World Finals on October 27, 2002. He never fully recovered from the injuries he sustained and passed away 14 months later.

Having left the Modified ranks behind in 1971, John Lingenfelter made his first final-round appearance in 1972 at Indy where his SS/NA Camaro took all the marbles with a 12.25. The Lingenfelter and Mike Meyer Camaro is seen here in 1973 warming the Firestones no doubt on its way to another victory. (Photo Courtesy Bob Martin)

After a few seasons running Pro Stock, John Lingenfelter returned to Super Stock in 1975. In his return, he won the season-opening Winternationals with this low-compression 350-powered 1973 Corvette. The car was the SS/LA record holder with an 11.38 at 117.18 when this 1976 Winternationals photo was shot. Running SS/MA, it was John's last event in the Charles Graf Corvette. He agreed to buy Tores's Chevy II prior to the race. (Photo Courtesy Dave Kommel)

Dick Hickernell and partner John Kring proved the LM1 255-hp 350 worked great in big packages as well. The Chevy was a record holder and played runner-up to John Lingenfelter at Indy in 1972. (Photo Courtesy Bob Martin)

Joe Scott

Joe Scott of Sunbury, Pennsylvania, was one of those Chevy racers who flew under the radar of many people as he went about his business and racked up the wins. He first drew attention at the 1970 Super Stock Nationals where his 1967 Camaro defeated the mighty Mopar of Ken Montgomery in the Super Stock final. Joe, a graduate of Division 1's fierce Junior Stock battles, had been sidetracked the year before with a broken back. Doctors told him he'd never walk again. However, strength, perseverance, and faith in God proved otherwise. He went on to be one of the most dominant Super Stock racers of the 1970s and 1980s.

Shortly after his Super Stock Nationals win, he picked up a 1969 Camaro ragtop. The car was an original Indy pace car that had been collecting dust in a friend's barn. With a little bargaining, the exchange of a few cases of beer, and a couple hundred bucks, the car was Joe's. In short order, the 396 and 4-speed was yanked, and in their place went a 255-hp 350 and turbo 400. The car debuted in 1971, and the combo fell nicely into SS/KA. He grabbed a number of division races before he won Super Stock at Indy in 1977. In 1978, he repeated as runner-up at the Grand-

nationals and won that summer's *Popular Hot Rodding* meet. He chased the points in 1980, won the Division 1 crown that year (and again in 1981), and closed the season as the Super Stock World Champion.

More national event wins followed: the Grandnationals in 1981, the Gators and Grandnationals in 1982, the Grandnationals again in 1989, and a runner-up finish at the Keystone Nationals in 1993. The Camaro was eventually sold to Billy Nees, who saw his own success with the car before he sold it to a bracket racer who, in Joe's words, "cut it up and turned it into junk." Joe's last ride was an SS/GT-TD Chevy S-10 that qualified number one everywhere it raced. A garage fire in 2000 destroyed the S-10, trailer, and equipment and pretty much wiped Joe out. His last trip down the track was in 2012.

Joe Scott's rise to fame started with this M/S Chevy wagon, seen here at 522 Dragway in Kreamer, Pennsylvania. Don't tell anyone, but at times Joe ran a 302 with 283 heads in the 4-speed-equipped wagon. (Photo Courtesy Carl Rubrecht)

This Camaro of Joe Scott started life as an L78-powered Indy Pace Car. With Joe at the wheel and a 350 under the hood, the Camaro saw more action on the track than it ever did on the street. Joe was voted to the Car Craft All-Star team in 1978 as the S/S driver. (Photo Courtesy Dave Kommel)

☆☆☆ THE BEST OF THE REST ☆☆☆

The possibilities to the Chevy racer in Super Stock (just as in Stock) were limitless because no other manufacturer offered such a multitude of combinations. Competition was tough in Super Stock, and the Chevy racers needed to be on their game to earn wins against Hemi Mopars and Cobra Jet Fords. These are a few more Chevy racers who made us proud.

Val Hedworth had hands of gold. No matter what he drove (Stocks to Super Stocks, Tri-Fives to Camaros), he came out a winner. Along with his own five national event wins and multiple national records, Val's Super Stock Engineering assisted many more before retiring in Missouri. (Photo Courtesy Dave Kommel)

Childhood friends Carl Bennett and Ron Sirianni joined forces on the track in 1971 to run Carl's Just Me Camaro. When that car crashed, this Camaro was built using the salvaged parts. Power came by way of a Truppi-Kling-built 295-hp 350. The car proved to be a killer in SS/I and was the first small-block Chevy-powered S/S car to crack the 10s. Ron did the deed at Englishtown in the spring of 1975 and recorded a 10.99. The Camaro ran a record-setting best of 10.72 while winning the Little Guy Nationals in 1975. (Photo Courtesy Bill Truby)

☆☆☆ THE BEST OF THE REST ☆☆☆

George Supinski ran a number of potent Chevys starting back in the early days of 1960s Junior Stock. In 1976, he won the NHRA Grandnationals with an SS/NA 1969 Camaro ragtop and repeated in 1980 behind the wheel of this 350-powered 1969 Corvette. Times in the 10.90s were the norm for this fiberglass bomb. (Photo Courtesy Bob Boudreau)

According to the NHRA, the winningest woman in racing is Amy Faulk, who won in three different categories. In 1979, Amy was wheeling this 1967 Camaro in SS/HA. Here, she's on the verge of defeating Bob Marshall to earn her first S/S national event win and the World Championship. She went into the books as the first woman to do so. (Photo Courtesy Dave Kommel)

Mike Boyle's Good Ol' Charlie Brown is a seven-time IHRA World Champion. Racing since 1970, Mike won his first championship in 1978. A single 4-barrel, 0.060-over 283 powered the wagon, and it was always a 4-speed and 12-bolt rear end. (Photo Courtesy Steve Reyes)

Jr. Thompson and his rough-and-ready B/Gas 1941 Studebaker was NHRA's first Little Eliminator champ, way back in 1958. Powered by a McCullough supercharged Chevy, this was the car that started the raging Gasser and cam wars. Thompson ran with an Isky. (Author's Collection)

Chapter Four

Sizzling Sportsmen

W e're talking about the categories known over the years as Street, Super, Modified, Comp, and Pro Comp Eliminators. As far as variety goes, you couldn't ask for more. Gassers, Altereds, and Modified production cars were always fan favorites, and are what we focus on here. The number of prevalent Chevys or Chevy-powered cars over the years in these categories are too numerous to mention. By the mid-1970s, there were 56 different classes to choose from. Of those classes, Chevy or Chevy-powered cars held approximately 66 percent of the class records.

Gas Explodes

Sanctioned drag racing came into being in 1955. It was a different world back then with Chrysler's Hemi battling for supremacy against everything from Ardun Flatheads to Rocket Oldsmobiles. But things changed quickly with the introduction of Chevy's compact V-8. Jr. Thompson and his rough-and-ready B/Gas 1941 Studebaker was NHRA's first Little Eliminator champ way back in 1958. Powered by a McCullough supercharged Chevy, this car started the raging Gasser Wars and Cam Wars that ran well into the 1960s. Thompson ran his Chevy with an Isky cam.

The NHRA's first World Points Champion was Buddy Garner of Hobbs, New Mexico, who amassed 500 points with his Chevy-powered C/A Plymouth in 1960. It was the first year of NHRA's points program, which ran April 3 to September 25. The NHRA implemented the program "in an effort to add more interest for those active in drag racing, regardless of their competition class or

The grand prize for Buddy Garner's points championship was a 1961 Chevy pickup equipped with a V-8 engine, oversize tires, heavy-duty springs, and topped with a custom camper manufactured by NHRA Safety Safari leader Bud Coons at his Kansas business. (Author's Collection)

There aren't many better looking Corvettes than "Big John" Mazmanian's Candy red 1961. John bought the car new with an injected 283 and raced it with help of Ford legend Earl Wade. The injectors soon gave way to a GMC 4-71 blower and the block opened to 316 ci. Sport Production wins were common. (Photo Courtesy John Foster Jr.)

Joe Mondello and Sush Matsubara campaigned this Ron Scrima Exhibition Engineering Fiat through 1969. The nitro-fed 427 made it the first Fuel Altered to run in the 7-second bracket. At the 1969 NHRA Nationals, Sush set the AA/FA record with a 7.24 at 213 mph. To put that into perspective, the low ET for Funny Car at the event was a 7.22 turned in by the Hemi Barracuda of Don Schumacher. (Photo Courtesy James Handy)

geographical location." Garner's *Flop* was powered by an Hilborn-injected 301-ci Chevy. Go-fast goodies included Jahns pistons, an Engle cam, and heads by McGurk. The mighty mouse was backed by a Chevy 3-speed transmission and a 4.89-geared Studebaker rear end.

Drag racing evolved quickly, and by the early 1960s, the Willys and Tri-Five Chevys were the popular choices in the numerous Eliminator brackets. Dominant cars that come to mind were those of John Loper and Gene Moody. John in his B/G, Chevy-powered 1941 Willys won class five times at national events between 1960 and 1963. And remember, this was when there were only two major events each year. Gene Moody had similar results with his D/G '55 Chevy between 1963 and 1967.

The Mallicoat Brothers

The popularity of turbocharging today owes a lot to Gary and Jerry Mallicoat. The twin brothers were the first to run turbos with any success, doing so back in 1965 when their twin turbo Chevy-powered Willys cleaned house at the NHRA Winternationals. The brothers, based in Gardena, California, began drag racing at the famed Lions Dragstrip with a naturally aspired Chevy-powered C/Gas 1940 Ford. Seeing the lighter, shorter wheelbase Willys as the way to go, they went hunting for one and found an original car close to home that a police officer used as his daily driver. The brothers were the proud owners of a 1941 Willys $400 later.

Through racing, the brothers became tight with Robert "Bones" Balogh, who allowed them to use his shop in Inglewood and helped them with the build. Bones donated the 283 from his own Chevy Gasser to the Willys and was the first to drive the brothers' car. The stout

> **"Needless to say, without Isky's help from the beginning, this project might never have happened. The turbos Garrett supplied the brothers for their 327 were experimental units, which were basically TE06 for aircrafts."**
> **– Jerry Mallicoat**

little mill mounted a GMC 6-71 and six Stromberg 97 carburetors, placing the car in C/Gas. The 283 was backed by a LaSalle box, but when Bones blew it up (nearly tearing the car in half), a B&M 4-speed Hydro was installed. A Chevy truck rear end with full-floating hubs and 5.12 gears filled the bill.

In 1963, the Mallicoats built their own blown 283 with an Isky blower drive, 505C camshaft, and Hilborn two-port injectors. They ran the combo into the fall of 1963 before it split a cylinder. In need of an engine for the upcoming 1964 Winternationals, they purchased a 300-hp 327 long-block from Iskenderian, who purchased a number of the engines from a local Chevy dealer. Along

The Mallicoats started with a stock Willys they purchased for $400 from a policeman in Westminster, California. To lighten the load, Cal Automotive fiberglass panels were added before the car was painted '56 Dodge Royal Blue Metallic. (Photo Courtesy Bones Balogh/Mallicoat Brothers Collection)

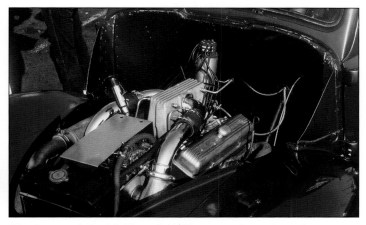

The heart of the Mallicoat's Willys was the twin turbo 327. Inners included Ansen pistons and rods, 9.25:1 compression, an Isky 505C cam, and gear drive. A Joe Hunt magneto lit the fire. With an abundance of torque produced by the turbocharged Chevy, the engine didn't need to rev so high, allowing for a switch from 5.12 to 4.56 rear gears. (Photo Courtesy Bones Balogh/Mallicoat Brothers Collection)

with the new engine came a move to B/GS. To further lighten the Willys, a fiberglass hood, fenders, doors, and decklid were added. The heavy truck rear end was replaced with an Olds rear, which was supported by a new quarter elliptic spring suspension.

With little time to prepare for the winter meet, mods to the 327 were limited. The dome of the stock pistons was shaved to lower compression, some side clearance was added to the stock rods, and an Isky cam and blower drive were used. The efforts paid off with a B/GS class win and their first national event trophy. Jerry said, "With the light pistons and rods, that engine would go to 9,000-plus rpm with no problems. We ran that engine until it was time to go back East on a match race tour against K. S. Pittman." They borrowed a 350-ci engine from friend Steve Fraze, and he and Jerry headed out on tour. Gary stayed home to rebuild the 327 and came out East with the fresh mill before the NHRA Nationals.

Ironically, Jerry had to race Bones Balogh, who was driving Big John Mazmanian's Willys in the semifinals. Bones ran faster, but Jerry used a hole shot to win by a matter of inches. On that run, a cylinder head cracked, and they were defeated by Jack Merkel in the final. The brothers ran the 327 through 1964 before they rebuilt it with Ansen rods and pistons for the twin-turbo setup.

The brothers began toying with the twin turbos late in 1964. Jerry, who worked for Isky part time while he went to school, recalled the day Bill Edwards from Cragar Industries rolled in with his twin turbo 231-ci Chevy. The engine was for a Bonneville car and he wanted to run it on the dyno.

"In comes a guy, Al Williams of Scientific Engineering out of Kansas. He was an engineer for North American Aviation and was renting a house from Iskenderian." Al put the brothers in touch with Duke Hallock, an engineer with Garrett. Al was instrumental in the turbo project and fabricated the stainless steel exhaust headers and modified the Corvette fuel-injection intake manifold.

The Mallicoat Willys was a real goer that backed up its performance with great looks. Jerry Mallicoat worked for Car Craft magazine during the mid-1960s and used his front yard for this photo shoot. (Photo Courtesy Bones Balogh/Mallicoat Brothers Collection)

At the Winternationals, the 3.82 first gear B&M Hydro helped Jerry Mallicoat get an early lead on Hugh Tucker in the Stone, Woods & Cook Willys. Five-foot-long ladder bars and Racemaster 10-inch slicks aided in traction. Jerry started his runs with the Hydro in second gear. (Photo Courtesy Gary and Jerry Mallicoat)

Needless to say, without Isky's help from the beginning, this project might never have happened. The turbos Garrett supplied the brothers for their 327 were experimental units, which were basically TE06 for aircrafts. According to Jerry, that was the closest they had for the size of stuff the brothers were running. Fuel came by way of a pair of Carter AFB carburetors fed through the '57 fuel-injection housing that served as the intake manifold.

On initial outings with the new setup, the brothers had trouble getting the boost up, so they talked to B&M, who made mods to the hydro torus members and got them up to 4,000 stall speed. With starting-line boost, coupled with the B&M's gear ratios, the Willys was nearly unbeatable off the line. In a dyno comparison between the roots engine and the twin turbo engine, the turbo engine's 720-hp output surpassed the roots engine by 130. Each engine ran 19 pounds of boost. Jerry said, "We definitely had an advantage when we went to the Winternationals."

At the winter meet, Jerry recalled defeating the C&O Hydro's Austin and Jr. Thompson before facing Hugh Tucker in the Stone, Woods & Cook hemi-powered Swindler B Willys in the B/GS final.

"Dougie was running the two cars, and he just ran the A car and couldn't get back to the start line in time, so they put Hugh Tucker behind the wheel. I can remember every foot of that run. Off the line, I carried the front wheels heading toward the centerline, I reached over and shifted the transmission, and it came down. Got it in high gear and looked over, and Tucker was on my quarter panel. There ain't no way he's going to out mile per hour me. I won the race and was so happy I was beating on the steer-ing wheel, and I went right past the finish line. Pomona being kind of short, I almost didn't get the car stopped." Jerry's winning time was a 10.59 at 135.55 mph.

After the Winternationals win, the brothers took the Willys on a whirlwind match race tour that lasted through the summer. By the fall, match race dates were getting harder to find, as the emerging Funny Cars were exploding in popularity. The quickest the Willys ran was at Salt Lake City, where Jerry recorded a 10.18 at 139 mph. At the time, everyone else was still in the 10.50 range. The turbo engine proved to be a reliable combination. Outside of tossing one of the Ansen rods after over-revving, breakage was never a problem.

After the summer tour, the brothers took a hiatus from racing and went back to school. The engine was pulled from the Willys and given to Iskenderian. The Willys was sold to a man in Huntington Beach who put a big-block Chevy in it. The last word was that the car was sitting in San Diego. After school, the brothers went on to further success and ran a few different twin turbo Hemi-powered Barracudas. The final one was a Pro Mod car with a Brad Anderson motor. This combination resulted in a 5-second ET with speeds near 250 mph. The brothers retired in 2017 after 55 years of racing.

Jack Merkel

Jack Merkel deserves a mention here for not only building what many considered to be the baddest 1933 Willys ever but also for his many contributions to the sport. Jack first made the scene at age 16 with a D/Gas '55 Chevy. His early success enabled him to open his own shop in 1959 in Ridgewood, New York. At Westhampton in May 1959, Jack earned four trophies: one for taking D/Gas, another

Jack's 1939 Willys ran a 368-ci Chevy (0.020 bore x 5/8 stroke). That earned him B/GS class wins at Indy in 1963 and 1964. In August 1964, he set the class record at Island Dragway with a 10.42 at 135.13 mph before he moved on to a new Willys. (Author's Collection)

Ferd Napfel's Gasser

erd Napfel's *Storming Bull* was another Tri-Five that stood out during the mid-1960s Gasser era. Ferd, who hailed from Catonsville, Maryland, called 75–80 his home track. He debuted his '55 in 1959 and went on to win class at the NHRA Nationals in 1964, 1965, and 1967. In 1965, he capped his class win with Street Eliminator honors and defeated Carl Kirk's Chevy-powered A/Gas Anglia with a 13.15 time.

Ferd was also an NHRA F and G/Gas record holder from 1964 through 1968, hitting the 12.90s at nearly 108 mph. That's not bad for a car that weighed over 4,000 pounds and ran nothing larger than 283-ci engines, according to his son. A one-piece A-1 fiberglass front clip took some weight off the front. Added weight was welded to the rear of the car, and twin tractor batteries were in the trunk. Hilborn injectors, a Sig Erson cam, 50-pound flywheel, and 8,000-rpm launches helped get the Chevy moving. A slick-shifted 4-speed was backed by a leaf-spring-mounted truck rear end with floating axles and welded gears. The mighty mouse was harnessed by a single traction arm fabricated by Ferd. The front suspension remained pretty much stock.

Ferd flat-towed the '55 to the Nationals in 1964, where he defeated Wes Edwards's E/G Poison Ivy *in Eliminations. Ferd's lone crew member was "Tate" Pruitt, who also helped with engine builds. Paul Houge at Racing Parts and Machine Co. in Baltimore did most of the machine work on the 283. (Photo Courtesy Forrest Bond)*

Ferd followed the Stormin' Bull *in 1969 with a 1964 Corvette dubbed* Super Bull. *Though the Corvette failed to obtain the same success as the '55, Ferd enjoyed running Gas with the car until his retirement in 1977. (Photo Courtesy Todd Wingerter)*

for setting the mile per hour record with a 92.18, and two more from winning B/Gas with an Olds-powered 1932 Chevy when he set the mile per hour record with a 97.29.

Jack's next venture was a 1939 Willys that he debuted in 1962. With 364 cubic inches of Chevy, the car was built to compete in the B/GS and was runner-up in class at

Indy in 1962, followed by wins in 1963 and 1964. Looking to compete with the heavy hitters in A/GS, Jack built a new, lighter 1933 Willys for 1965. Running the same 364, Jack took class at Indy that year and defeated the SOHC Ford-powered Willys of the supposedly unbeatable Ohio George Montgomery. The Willys topped 148 mph

Jack's 427 incorporated aluminum heads and a GMC 6-71 blower topped with a Hilborn fuel injection and bug catcher. The Willys rode on Halibrand quick-mount rims up front and 10-inch American Torque Thrusts out back. Jack's Merkel Performance gave rise to numerous winners across the nation. (Author's Collection)

The gold metal-flake paint covering the restored all-fiberglass Willys body matches the original chartreuse yellow that Charlie Doerkin applied way back when. As of this writing, the restored Willys is in the hands of Ron Normann, who happens to own Jack's restored 1939 Willys as well. (Photo Courtesy Chadly Johnson)

before Jack retired the car at the end of 1966 to make way for a new car in 1967.

And what a car it would be! The new Willys featured an all-fiberglass shell, a 3-inch top chop, a fiberglass decklid, fenders, and a one-piece lift-off front end. Subtle mods, such as a flush-mounted windshield, molded fenders, and a channeled body, were all incorporated to help cheat the wind. Charlie Doerkin sprayed on a heavy metallic, chartreuse yellow paint while Jack assembled the 427 Chevy. Jack incorporated aluminum heads, a GMC 6-71 blower topped with Hilborn fuel injection, and a bug catcher. He worked close with Crower Cams and trialed numerous shafts. Frank Cali performed a lot of the fabrication work on the new car, including boxing the stock 1933 frame rails. Behind the 427 was a Vitar

Turbo 400 and a 1960 Oldsmobile rear end that housed 4.56 gears. The rear was supported with coilover shocks, a panhard bar, and a unique traction arm of Jack's own design that was based loosely on a 1940s Jaguar design.

A graduate of Pratt Institute, Jack based his thesis on the arm and came up with a mathematical equation that worked flawlessly. It goes like this: the length of the bar/arm divided by the rear gear ratio equals the distance between the driveshaft and the tip of the torque arm. If you deviated from this theory, the bar wasn't as effective.

Ready to race, the Willys weighed in at a meager 2,135 pounds. Before he retired the Willys in 1969 to focus on his family and business, Jack propelled the car to a best of 8.75 seconds at 160 mph.

The Trio Known as *Mister Crude*

Rydell, Hope, and Lang were a trio of mid-class Gassers who teamed up in 1967. For the next few years, they campaigned a G/G Anglia affectionately known as *Mister Crude*. Rydell had the idea sometime after Indy 1967 to improve the breathing of their 292-ci 6-cylinder by chopping the ends off of a pair of small-block Chevy heads and welding the remaining six chambers together. The deed worked because the bore spacing of the 6-cylinder and V-8 were nearly identical.

The intake for the new design came courtesy of a modified V-8 Crower injection. The trio is believed to be the first to use V-8 heads on a 6-cylinder, and the experiment really paid off. The Anglia went from low-11 elapsed times to 10.79 and held the class record for what seemed like forever.

At the 1969 NHRA Springnationals, the newly formed heads won the trio the Best Engineered Car award. Of course, imitation being the sincerest form of flattery, it wasn't long before every 6-cylinder drag car seemed to be sporting modified V-8 heads.

Rydell, Hope, and Lang turned slicing and dicing V-8 heads onto 6-cylinders into a winning art form. The heads first appeared on their class-winning Mr. Crude G/Gas Anglia back in 1969. The engine was transplanted into a Vega and then into this Altered during the summer of 1972. Note the front-mounted magneto. (Photo Courtesy Bob Boudreau)

Seibert and Bugenski

And speaking of raging sixes, Bob Seibert and John Bugenski pretty much had the lower Gas classes covered in the mid-1970s with their 6-cylinder-powered Vega. Starting with a wrecked Vega they bought from Schram's Auto Parts in Pontiac, Michigan, the pair went to work over the winter of 1972–1973 to build the terror. Power came courtesy of a GMC 302 inline-6 bored out 0.125 and de-stroked using a 248 crank. Final displacement was 306 ci. To make up for the shorter stroke, the block was decked 3/16 of an inch. Go-fast goods included Hooker headers and a fabricated intake mounted with Weber carbs. C. J. Batten was called on to rework the production head, opening the ports to the extent that water leaks

would be an ongoing issue.

Seibert said, "C. J. wanted to take two heads, cut one low through the ports and one high through the ports and weld them back together, but the NHRA wouldn't allow it. Class requirements stated it had to be a production head."

A General Kinetics flat-tappet cam that featured 310–320 duration really made the six come alive. Compression was a maximum of 10.5:1, and Seibert readily admits there was room for improvement there. Pistons swung on aluminum Hemi rods. Dynamic Speed Center in Detroit was called on to do the machine work. "They hated to see me coming in. To take 3/16 off the deck took the better part of the day." Due to ongoing breakage

Seibert and Bugenski had their work cut out for them in making the 6-cylinder Vega a Modified winner. The 248 crank had to be replaced every 30 runs or so because it would crack between the number-6 rod journal and the rear main. Additional bolts were added to retain the flywheel, and epoxy glue was used to ensure they didn't come loose. The crank end was drilled for a larger 5/8-inch aircraft bolt (and epoxied) to retain the harmonic balancer. (Photo Courtesy Bob Martin)

Bob Seibert smiles for the camera while partner John Bugenski is busy on the Jimmy six. The pair's J/Gas 1967 Camaro ran mid to low 13s in 1970. The 306-ci featured Weber down drafts, Elkin-prepped heads, fabricated headers, and a heck of a lot of ingenuity. (Photo Courtesy Bob Seibert)

New panels were hung on the Vega prior to 1975 and tangerine paint was applied. The Vega was voted Best Appearing Sportsman car at the season-ending Division 5 banquet. It was the same year Seibert and Bugenski won the division points title. (Photo Courtesy Bob Boudreau)

issues, everything up top was fabricated: rockers, rocker shaft, and stands.

Originally a wide-ratio Muncie backed the six before the pair swung a deal with Doug Nash in 1974 for one of his 5-speed transmissions. It seems Doug loved his train sets and Seibert happened to have a Lionel set he wanted. The pair traded straight up. Bob rowed the Hurst through the Nash gears at 6,500 rpm. The rear end was an early Olds with 5.38 gears supported by modified Mopar S/S springs. It was around 1974 when Seibert had Wolverine Chassis redo the front suspension. Newer style body panels were installed at the same time.

Between 1972 and 1975, the team won the Division 3 title twice, took class at the Springnationals four times, the Gators twice, the Summernationals three times, the Sportsnationals twice, and the U.S. Nationals three times. National event final eliminator wins came in 1974 (Gators and Summer) and 1975 (Summernationals). In 1973, Bob was voted the top Sportsman driver. Before he retired at the end of 1975, Bob dropped the N and J/Gas records numerous times and ran as quick as 11.47. The Vega was sold to a guy in Rochester, New York, and disappeared after a while.

Ralph Ridgeway

The NHRA debuted its Modified Production category in 1964 and it was an instant hit. The category was created for those who wanted to modify their Stockers but not to the extent of all-out Gassers. One of the first stars of the category was Ralph Ridgeway and his '55 Chevy.

Ralph purchased the car in 1964 as a project someone else gave up on.

Over the next few years, he used the car to rewrite both the NHRA and AHRA record books. He ran the car in C and D/MP through 1968 as well as AHRA F1 and F2/ Hot Rod. He won class at Indy in 1965 and went on a tear in 1966 when he won 27 of 28 races and took Street Eliminator honors 15 times at New England and the surrounding area tracks. In 1967, he won class at the NHRA Springnationals, Indy, and the AHRA Nationals. The car was a holy terror in AHRA where on July 1, 1967, Ralph set 10 class records at his home track in New England. His best time with the '55 was 11.66 at 118.80 mph. Not bad for a 301-powered car that weighed a little over 3,300 pounds.

The heart of the Chevy was the punched-out 283 that mounted a tunnel-ram-style intake manifold of Ralph's own design. Working with sponsor Carl Debien of Deb's Automotive, Ralph trialed the latest cross ram manifold design but found it lacked the desired top-end power when compared to even the conventional twin 4-barrel intake.

Ralph said, "Carl and I determined that the cross-ram runners were too long for effective high-RPM horsepower. So we started looking at what else was available to come up with a shorter runner. We settled on a Chevrolet fuel-injection manifold to which we modified the runner lengths and the inside of the plenum chamber to suit the use of carburetors. The original fuel-injection unit only had air introduced into the plenum, not an air/fuel

Ralph Ridgeway's '55 saw action in both AHRA and NHRA competition. Noted on the quarter panel are the nine AHRA records Ralph set in one day. The 301-ci engine really showed the possibilities of running a small-inch, high-winding Chevy. (Author's Collection)

Twin Carters carbs are mounted atop Ralph Ridgeway's home-designed Ridge Runner manifold. Ralph's intake was based upon a factory fuel-injection unit and gave the Chevy the top end charge Ralph was looking for. Notice that the car retains its windshield wiper motor. Modified rules of the day dictated that it remain in place. (Author's Collection)

Lightweight buckets kept Ralph secure as he rowed the unbreakable Hurst shifter through the gears. Gauges, tach, and a brake hold was all that was needed as the trip was done in little more than 12.5 seconds. (Author's Collection)

Ralph followed his Bel Air with this mouse-motored 1969 Z28. The Camaro set a few records and made a great mobile lab for Ralph's ongoing parts development. Running a 311-ci engine here, the Camaro ran consistent 11.50s times. A 40-pound flywheel, slick-shifted Muncie, and 5.57 gears got the Camaro out in a hurry. (Author's Collection)

mixture. We then machined a suitable top plate to mount the AFB carburetors I was using at the time. The car was instantly 0.1 to 0.2 seconds and 2 mph quicker."

Shortly afterward, Ralph switched to Holley carbs that he mounted sideways to make removal of the float bowls for jet changes much easier. With the ability to switch top plates and going from twin carbs to a single carb, Ralph was able to destroy the record books that July day at New England. Additional ponies for the 301 came by way of a Crane cam, Mondello heads, a Wico ignition, and owner-fabricated headers.

In 1968, Ralph started selling his Ridge Runner Ram manifold and eventually sold several hundred copies. He recalled at the Nationals that year Grumpy Jenkins came by with Edelbrock and took a good look at the manifold. In short order, Edelbrock had its own version, the tunnel ram manifold, on the market. At the end of the 1968 season, the '55 was sold to someone in Quebec, Canada, where it was crashed not long after.

In 1969 and 1970, Ralph campaigned a 1969 Camaro out of Norwood Chevrolet of Warwick, Rhode Island. He ran NHRA Super Stock, E/Gas, D/Gas, and AHRA, where he set the E/HR class record at New England on August 2, 1970, when he ran an 11.46. His last race car was a 1970½ Camaro that recorded a best of 10.90 at 125 mph. In IHRA F1 FMS, Ralph lowered the 1/8 mark with a 7.60.

Though Ralph was out of the driver's seat, he continued to design his own aftermarket parts. In late 1973, he designed a rocker stud support similar to the Jomar Girdle that allowed valve adjustments without the use of U-bolts. The Stud Support was the first marketed product under Ridgeway Racing Associates, a company that began in 1973 and continues to operate today by manufacturing numerous performance parts.

Carroll Caudle

In the same breath as Ralph Ridgeway, you could mention a dozen other '55s. Another standout that can't be ignored is the Bel Air of Carroll Caudle. Carroll seemed to have a thing for '55s. He ran a pair of them before he burned a blaze through Modified Production with the one pictured here. Carroll, with his wife Gwenda as his crew chief, raced his Bel Air into the early 1970s, and set in the neighborhood of 20 class records and won the inaugural Modified Eliminator world title in 1970. Carroll held nothing back at the World Finals, where—running F/Gas with a 310-ci engine under the hood—the Bel Air ran a record-setting 11.83, defeating the redlighting

Division 4 hall of famer Carroll Caudle bought his Bel Air off its original owner and raced it in classes from C/MP down to G/MP with small-blocks he built by boring, stroking, and de-stroking. His world title in 1970 went along with a Division 4 championship, which is something he won numerous times through his career. (Photo Courtesy Tom Ordway)

B/Dragster of Dave Armbruster. The World Finals win proved very beneficial to Carroll, who saw business at his Carroll's Performance Engines company explode. His long-lasting reputation is behind his thriving business to this day.

Although Carroll tried his hand in Pro Stock with a 1968 Camaro and later raced a Don Hardy–built Modified Eliminator Vega, the '55 is the car he is best remembered for. He'd run the car in classes C/MP down to G/MP with engines of various sizes built by his own hands. He set his first class record in C/MP back in September 1968 at 11.69 with a 301-ci buzzing well over 8,000 rpm. Backing the various engines was a slick-shifted BorgWarner and a slapper bar–controlled Tri-Five rear housing. Propelling the 3,100-plus pound shoebox to record times were parts by Racer Brown and Crane. Holley carbs were initially mounted on a modified cross ram intake. Carroll felt there was too much plenum for the small-cubic-inch engine and partially filled and contoured the inners with epoxy. In similar fashion to Ralph Ridgeway, Carroll replaced the cross ram with a tunnel ram manifold of his own design with a 1962 Corvette fuel-injection unit as the base.

Carroll's design worked so well that Edelbrock asked to borrow it to assist in the design of its own tunnel ram manifold. Carroll tested the manufacturer's version but reportedly felt the intake never measured up to his design, which the manufacturer failed to return to him. Those old enough may recall those early Edelbrock tunnel ram manifolds had a huge plenum. Ed Wright, a longtime friend of Carroll, recalled seeing one Carroll had about half-filled with fiberglass resin.

Carroll Caudle forsook his trusted '55 Bel Air in 1973 to run this Don Hardy Vega. The Vega ran both B/MP and F/G. Multiple division wins in 1973 had Carroll falling just short of division champ, which was won by Lee Shepherd. (Photo Courtesy Dave Kommel)

Carroll still owns the '55 and occasionally takes it to special events. That is when he can find the time. The man has barely missed a step over the years and continues to operate Carroll's Performance Engines in Amarillo.

Scotto and Blevins

The Joe Scotto and Paul Blevins story begins like many others: two high school chums decided to pool their resources and go drag racing. Recalling their early days, Joe said, "Paul and I were there when the Napps were clearing the forest for Englishtown Raceway. That's when we made the decision to go drag racing." It was 1966 and their category of choice was Modified Eliminator. They scrounged the scrapyards for the ideal candidate and came up with a $50 Nomad. The car needed little more than a few fenders that Joe replaced before laying on the white paint. While Paul was in Turkey serving Uncle Sam and reading all the American car magazines he could get his hands on, Joe was at home preparing the wagon.

The pair initially relied on a warmed-over 327 to do battle but got nowhere until they hooked up with Danny Jesel and the guys at Duffy's. The year was 1968, and with

The Scotto-Blevins Nomad was an unbeatable record holder in both the AHRA and NHRA. In UDRA competition, the car practically owned the Modified Circuit. Paul dropped his own G/MP class record to 11.44 before he retired the car in 1972. (Photo Courtesy Carl Rubrecht)

Danny Jesel did the machining on the Scotto-Blevins 283, while Blevins did the final assembly. Their 9,000-rpm launches were the norm, and as Joe recalled, "We only broke one engine." (Photo Courtesy Bob Dastalto)

a fresh 0.030-over 283, the Nomad was bringing home the gold more times than not. Feeling one driver would get to know the car better than two and improve consistency, it was decided that Paul would be the permanent driver. He set his first record in G/MP at York in June 1968 and ran a 12.16. He retained the record through 1972 and reset it twice.

Though the 283 could rev to 10,000 rpm and usually came off the line at 9,000 rpm, the engine and drivetrain were remarkably reliable and rarely broke. The 283 was

Scotto-Blevins's 1967 Corvette won the 1971 Supernationals, 1972 U.S. Nationals, and 1972 World Finals before the car was retired. A four-link Pontiac rear end helped ensure bulletproof launches. (Photo Courtesy Bob Boudreau)

Blevins, seen here at the Grandnationals at Sanair in 1974, updated his 1973 Vega with new panels prior to the season-opening Winternationals. Paul found life in Pro Stock a little tougher than in the Modified ranks. His biggest win in the Vega was at the Super Stock Nationals in 1973. (Photo Courtesy Bob Boudreau)

Paul Blevins's last go-round in Pro Stock came in 1977 behind the wheel of this SRD Monza. Though national event wins in Pro Stock escaped him, Paul was a serious threat until the end. Paul was never far from the sport, and he reemerged a number of years later with his son running a Junior Dragster. (Photo Courtesy Michael Pottie)

backed by a slick-shifted BorgWarner 4-speed that featured a 2.54 first gear, while out back an unbreakable '57 Olds rear end housed Summers axles and anywhere from 5.12 to 6.17 gears. An Air-Lift bag mounted on the right rear aided traction along with traction bars modified by Paul.

The Nomad was a consistent winner, so the pair was hounded by sponsors who wanted their name on the car. Joe said, "This led to plenty of free parts and directly to us building the World Championship–winning Corvette." Bill Izykowski was hired to drive the Corvette that took runner-up at the World Finals in 1971 before it won the following season. Joe retired from racing in 1972 to focus on his car sales business and gave both cars to Paul. Each was eventually sold to help finance Paul's Pro Stock effort.

Paul moved into Pro Stock in 1973 with an SRD-built Vega. He got off to a great start and won the Super Stock Nationals that year and the Division 1 points champion. Though national event wins eluded Paul in his Pro Stock effort, for a time he was considered the number-two Chevy guy behind Jenkins. He retired from active participation in drag racing in 1977 after campaigning an SRD Monza.

Reher, Morrison, Cross, and Shepherd

The team of David Reher and Buddy Morrison was a dominating force in Modified and later in Pro Stock. They first met as students at the University of Texas. In 1971, the budding drag racers started Reher-Morrison Racing Engines in the back room of an auto supply store in Mansfield, Texas. That same year, the pair teamed with Bobby Cross and supplied Cross with a small-block Chevy for the Maverick he and his father purchased new for the sole purpose of drag racing. The guys ran the Maverick in multiple Modified Production classes and set their first record in D/MP at Amarillo in 1971 with a 10.98 ET.

Aside from the Maverick, Morrison also owned an F/MP 1964 Chevy II station wagon that Lee Shepherd drove to a runner-up finish in Modified Eliminator at the 1972 NHRA Springnationals. For a brief period, the four gentlemen raced the two cars simultaneously. However, when Cross decided to take a hiatus from the sport shortly after the 1972 Springnationals, the Chevy II was parked and Shepherd took over driving the Maverick. In 1973, their efforts paid off when they won the Division 4 points championship. In 1974, the NHRA banned the hybrid car/engine combination from Modified, which forced the team to move the Maverick into the Gasser

A Chevy mill in a Ford Maverick you say? Well yeah, and Cross, Reher & Morrison made it work to the tune of record-setting 10.60 times. The hybrid Maverick was much feared in Modified Production before rule changes in 1974 saw a move to Gas. (Photo Courtesy Tommy Shaw)

Bobby Cross and Bubba Corzine

Bobby Cross returned in a big way in 1978 to run the A/Econo Dragster with teammate Bubba Corzine. Their Lester Gullory–chassis car counted on a Reher-Morrison 302-ci engine to win both the Summernationals and World Finals. The pair ran A, B, and C classes through 1980, and won a total of eight national events. A rule change over the winter of 1979–1980 saw the mouse motors booted from A/ED, so the pair headed to B/ED with a new superlight Don Ness car powered by a 338-ci Reher-Morrison engine. A return to A/ED mid-season saw Cross record 7.40 times with a Reher-Morrison 380-ci big-block. After they had their use of the car, it was sold at the end of the 1980 season to two brothers in Minnesota.

In 1980, the NHRA made A/ED a big-block-only class so Cross-Corzine de-stroked its 362-ci small-block to 338 ci and ran B/ED. It returned to A/ED for the last five races of the year and won the Fallnationals. (Photo Courtesy Steve Reyes)

ranks. In F/G at the Winternationals, Shepherd won Modified Eliminator when he defeated the Mopar of Jim Marshall in the final with a record-setting 10.39 at 130.62 mph.

The Maverick was sold for a hefty $6,000 after the Winternationals and the team debuted its 331-powered E/G 1967 Corvette (the former Raymond Martin and Hokie Holcomb car) at the Gatornationals. Shepherd won several WCS races through 1975 and ran a 10.40 at 129.87 mph to play runner-up at the Springnation-

als that year. Reher-Morrison parted with the Corvette at the end of the 1975 season and sold it to Tony Christian, who ran the car in G and H/Gas to win the 1976 Sportsnationals, Summernationals, and Grandnationals, plus the 1977 Winternationals.

Jack Trost

A Modified star of the 1970s, Jack Trost's keen interest in going fast was nurtured by his father Jim, who had him racing midget cars at age 8. By trade, "Big" Jim was

The name Mr. Fuzz was Jack Trost's son's nickname because the little guy only had a slight covering of fuzz on his head. Jack's Modified '55 was powered by a 0.060-over 283. (Photo Courtesy Michael Pottie)

The Trosts also ran their C/A Camaro in A/MP and Pro Stock with tunnel-rammed 427s by both Jenkins and Traco. Jack set eight National records and garnered three Wallys through his career. (Photo Courtesy Michael Pottie)

After rule changes bumped his first Vega from Modified Production, Jack Trost moved into Gas. He purchased Dave Strickler's old Vega, which suited the category better due to its relocated firewall and setback engine. Jack debuted the new Vega at the Sportsnationals in 1974. (Photo Courtesy Michael Pottie)

a body man and worked at Kirk Chevrolet in Newtown Square, Pennsylvania, before he opened his own shop and taught Jack the trade.

The pair chose to go drag racing in 1967 and built a C/MP 302-powered '55 Chevy. *Mr. Fuzz,* named for Jack's son, didn't set the world on fire but it wet the pair's feet and gave Jack much-needed experience on the strip. Follow-up efforts included a 1968 Camaro and a 1970 Nova that were run in numerous categories. Powering each *Ratified* car was a Jenkins Competition–prepared big-block.

The world-beating Modified Production Vega that we all know and love followed in 1973. The car dominated the class with its Jenkins Competition 331, set the record seven different times, and won C/MP class at the Summernationals in 1974. That same year Jack drove the car to Modified runner-up at Indy in D/G and recorded 9.80 times.

The SRD car was so dominant that the NHRA changed the minimum wheelbase rule and forced Jack to run the car as a Gasser. Not able to take full advantage of the Gas rules, Jack sold the car and purchased Dave Strickler's Pro Stock Vega. The Strickler Vega featured lighter weight construction and a relocated firewall, which allowed Jack to take advantage of the Gas class 10-percent engine setback rule. He sold the car after one season but continued to drive it for the new owner. He purchased one more

SRD Vega, the old Grumpy's *Toy X,* in 1978 before he retired from racing in 1981.

Jack was a real grassroots-style racer who frequented his home track of Maple Grove with family and friends as crew. In the mid-1970s, he took over his dad's body shop and renamed it the Fender Mender. Over the years, Trost painted cars for a number of racers, including Roger Penske (starting with his first-gen Camaros), Jenkins, Blevins, Shafiroff, and Bob Glidden. In 1988, Jack's life was cut short way too soon in a car crash.

Keener and Mercure

When it came to Camaros in the modified ranks, none were better than the cars campaigned by Mike Keener and Paul Mercure. The two first teamed up in 1973 and are still going strong today. Theirs is a long story that reads like a who's who of famed Michigan area racers. Paul, or "Merc" as he is affectionately known, had been running a C/MP 1967 Camaro as far back as 1970 and was a patron of Booth-Arons, the famed engine building duo. Keener became serious about racing in 1967 when he debuted his Butch Elkins–built D/A 1965 Corvette at the famed Motor City Dragway. On Keener's first trip to the track, he pitted next to Richard Maskin. Little did Mike know the influence Maskin would have on his career. The pair became close friends, and later that fall they were assigned to the same dorm in college.

In 1970, Dick Maskin and Mike Keener built this Camaro, which initially carried blue and white paint. Keener was drafted before the car was finished so Maskin ran it. Mike sold his interest to Jim Gilbert in 1971, and that was when it received its Wally Booth green and Mouse Pack 1 label. Maskin won Modified at the PHR meet in 1972 with a 10.88. (Photo Courtesy Bob Martin)

In 1968, they teamed up to campaign Maskin's C/MP '55 Canadian Pontiac. It was through Richard that Mike met Dick Arons. Arons was already considered famous for winning the 1967 and 1968 Super Stock Nationals. The Michigan racers were a tight-knit group, and in 1969 Maskin jumped at the chance to run Super Stock with Arons. Mike then took on Dave Kanners to run the D/A Corvette.

Late in the season, Maskin returned from the Arons camp, and armed with newfound knowledge, he and Mike set out to build their own Camaro. By March 1970, their blue and white 1968 was complete and ready for C/MP action. They couldn't have asked for a better start. That year, the Keener & Maskin Camaro became the first C/MP car to run in the 10s. Later, they set the national record at Indy with a 10.96 at 125.96 mph and it won the class.

It was around this time that Mike got a call from Uncle Sam. He sold his interest in the Camaro to Jim Gilbert, and it was at this time the car was christened

The **Check Mate** *Camaro, seen here in 1973, sported flames before the team debuted a new blue and white Camaro in 1974. Mercure took C/MP at the Nationals with a 10.63. The team of Keener-Mercure closed the season with the class record at 10.32. Not bad for 331 ci in a 3,400-pound car. (Photo Courtesy Bob Martin)*

The first **Check Mate** *Camaro was a revolutionary car by comparison to any other Modified Production car in 1974. Running B/MP and recording 9.90 times, the car has been described as an all-steel Pro Stocker. (Photo Courtesy Bob Martin)*

Mouse Pack 1 and painted green to match Wally Booth's Pro Stock *Rat Pack 1* Pro Stock Camaro.

Upon Mike's return from service in 1972, he had a Dick Maskin–prepared 1968 COPO Camaro and a sponsorship deal waiting for him. He initially ran the Camaro in SS/L with a 255-hp 350 then in SS/D with a 425-hp 427 in 1973. The Camaro ran consistently under the national record for both years.

It was around this time that Mike first met Mercure, and the pair became acquainted at Milan. They became good friends, and at Maskin's suggestion, they teamed up at the end of the 1973 season. Each of them sold their Camaros, and they started fresh in 1974 with the ex–John Lukovich A/MP Camaro. Mike Fons is credited for setting the Camaro up to run C/MP. Keener and Mercure agreed they would keep the *Check Mate* name Paul was

The **Check Mate** *Vega* was the second car built by SRD back in 1972 and was originally campaigned by Carmen Rotunda. Mike Fons updated the car for Keener-Mercure in 1975, and the biggest change was a switch from a three-link rear suspension to ladder bars. Mike Keener is pictured putting that suspension to work at the 1977 Winternationals. (Photo Courtesy Dave Kommel)

using, and to use the blue and white paint scheme Mike had originally developed while racing with Maskin.

Mike referred to the years 1974, 1975, and 1976 as magical. With Merc behind the wheel of the former Lukovich car, the pair notched its first NHRA Modified Eliminator win at the 1974 NHRA Sportsnationals. At the time, the Camaro was considered nothing short of revolutionary, and some labeled it as an all-steel Pro Stock. Powered by a Pro Stock–style 331-ci backed by a Chrysler 4-speed, the Camaro ran a four-link rear suspension, which the NHRA declared illegal immediately after the Sportsnationals win. It seems the sticking point was that the four-link was located outside of the frame rails. The Camaro was run as an E/Gasser through the end of the season at which point Fons replaced the four-link with a ladder bar setup.

After Paul's victory, the team built a second Camaro for Mike, who was eager to get back behind the wheel. Mike's Camaro, a D/MP 1968 powered by a 314-ci engine, qualified number 2 at the *Popular Hot Rodding* meet in August 1974 and won the eliminator. The pair's success carried over into 1975. Mike won the C/MP class at the Gatornationals and made it to the quarterfinals before he was eliminated. In April, Merc's Camaro became the first 9-pound-per-cubic-inch car to run in the 9s and set the E/G record at Columbus with a 9.98. At the proceeding Summernationals, each of them won class with both cars running in the 9s.

The pair debuted a C/Gas Vega in October 1975. With a 331-ci engine out of the Camaro, the former Carman Rotunda Pro Stocker set the class record in November with a 9.21 at 148.50 mph. A switch to a 292-ci in 1976 moved the little Vega into D/Gas. Keener did a fine job

behind the wheel and made the semifinals at the NHRA Springnationals and Grandnationals before he qualified number 1 and won Modified Eliminator at the Fallnationals. In 1977, Paul hitched a ride in the G/Gas Corvette of David Surles and made consecutive final-round appearances at the 1977 Springnationals and Summernationals. In 1978, Merc dusted off the trusty original 1967 Fons-built Camaro and took class at the 1978 Cajun Nationals and 1980 Sportnationals.

Paul and his D/MP Camaro came within a heartbeat of winning the final Modified championship in 1981, the only year that the title was determined by a season-long points chase. He won the Sportsnationals and Golden Gate Nationals, and he was runner-up to Larry Kopp at the Grandnationals, Summernationals, and World Finals.

The championship came down to the last round of the last Modified race. If Mercure had defeated Kopp, he would have snatched both the Modified championship and the lucrative Quaker State Sportsman Cup from Mike Edwards's grasp. Well, it just wasn't meant to be. The shifter in Paul's Camaro picked an inopportune time to go south, leaving him the best seat in the house to watch Kopp take the race.

After the NHRA pulled the plug on Modified Eliminator, the Keener-Mercure Camaro moved to Competition eliminator, won the World Finals, and posted runner-up finishes at the Gatornationals and the Northstar Nationals. Keener and Mercure made a brief foray into Pro Stock following the introduction of the 500-ci formula in 1983 but returned to their roots after a few season with a series of Camaro Stockers.

These guys just kept on, and kept on winning. By 1993 they had three Camaros in their stable, which were

Diving into Pro Stock, the team purchased this Don Ness Olds Ciera from Andy Mannarino and ran it from 1984 to 1986. Paul Mercure manned the Lenco. They tried another kick at Pro Stock in 1989 with a Don Ness Camaro but gave it up in 1991. (Photo Courtesy Allen Tracy)

driven by Mike, Merc, and Mark Yamarino. Running A, B, and C/Stock, the team continued to win class and divisional meets and set records. During one point in 1998 and 1999, Mike drove their 1968 Camaro to seven consecutive B/S class wins. Shortly after that, Mike got together with IHRA's Terry Bell and developed the idea for Top Stock, a heads-up category for A, B, and C/Stockers. The *Check Mate* team eventually won 11 Top Stock titles.

Giving credit where it's due, Mike is quick to note the helping hands of Tom Stiel and Jeff Jones. With these two in the pits, Keener-Mercure has continued its winning ways. Today, a 2015 COPO Camaro and an old A/S 1967 are getting the job done.

Cotton Perry

Jay Cotton Perry and his H/MP 1967 Chevy II proved that six in a row does go. Perry relied on his uncle and partner Jim Headrick to build the 301-ci six that turned Modified on its ear through the mid-1970s. With a reported 620 hp that propelled the car to eventual 10.60 times, Perry's reign of terror began in 1975 when he won the NHRA Division 2 crown. He and Headrick backed it up in 1976 and won the Gatornationals along the way. Their best year was in 1978, when they won three out of four Division 2 races, which earned them another division title. That same year, they also won Modified at the NHRA Sportsnationals, Cajun Nationals, Grandnationals, Honest Charley Stars & Stripes Open in Atlanta, and the PHR meet in Michigan.

There's no such thing as an ugly Chevy, but SS&DI magazine rated this the ugliest drag car due to its poor decal arrangement. Perry-Headrick first teamed on a 6-cylinder-powered 1964 Chevy II. They followed up with a 1966 hardtop before they built the Pocket Rocket in 1975. Pat Curron initiated the build. (Photo Courtesy Larry Pfister)

There were so many heavy hitters in Modified that to compete on the national level, you really had to be on your game. Cotton Perry and his screaming Chevy II sure were. Cotton is caught in action here at Bandimere in 1978 during the peak of his run in Modified. (Photo Courtesy Dave Kommel)

Dennis Ferrara owned A/MP with this rompin' stompin' 466-ci Baldwin-Motion Phase III Camaro. Although national event victory eluded the 3,300-pound car, class wins were common, and Dennis set and reset the class record numerous times. (Photo Courtesy Michael Pottie)

The 301 was stuffed with gas-ported Venolia pistons and topped with a Kay Sissell–modified cylinder head. Compression was 14.5:1. Weber carbs were initially incorporated before the pair made a switch to three Holley 550-cfm carbs on an aluminum intake fabricated by Headrick. A Cam Dynamics shaft featuring 0.900 lift actuated the valves. The deuce revved 10,800–11,000 rpm off the line and was shifted at 7,200 rpm.

Running up to 60 rounds per month, the 301 went through heads and rings at a regular rate. Initially, they might have had 25 runs out of the engine before it cracked a crank or pulled the webbing out of that block. Aluminum rods were added to help absorb some of the damaging shock, which necessitated grinding the block for clearance and dimpling the oil pan to clear the rod caps. According to Perry, they could then run a crank the full season. The little screamer was backed by a 27-pound flywheel and a 3.45 first gear, Doug Nash 5-speed. A Dana third member supported by a four-link carried either 5.57 or 5.88 gears.

With the death of Modified Eliminator in 1981, Perry briefly tried Super Stock in 1982 before he retired. Perry and Headrick resurfaced in Comp between 1984 and 1986 and teamed with Brian Browell. With a Headrick engine and Perry at the controls they won two national events.

The Chevy II was sold to Danny Davis sometime around 1986, and as Danny recalled, the only thing left from the *Pocket Rocket* when they purchased it was the roof, doors, quarter panels, and some flooring. Danny

rebuilt the car with a 275-hp 327 that fit perfect in SS/HA. With Ross Wilson at the wheel, the Chevy II became the first SS/HA car to run 9.90 and 9.80 elapsed times. It took another year before any other car in class ran a 9.80 time.

Dennis Ferrara

Dennis Ferrara set the record books on fire in Modified and Comp Eliminator with everything from Camaros to an Econo Altered rail. His cars were the scourge to many and the envy of most. Dennis paid his dues in Stock before he joined forces with Joel Rosen, his boss at Motion Performance, to run an A/MP 1971 Camaro. When they tore into the Baldwin-Motion SS454 car, the pair started by acid dipping all of the removable pan-

> **"Although we owned the class, the [Camaro] was heavy and broke a lot of parts. Rosen received an offer on the car that he just couldn't refuse, and off to Hawaii it went."**
>
> **– Dennis Ferrara**

els. Into the vacant engine bay went 466 cubic inches of tunnel-rammed big-block. The car was an immediate success and set the class record in May 1972 with a time of 10 seconds flat. By the following season, Dennis had dropped the record to 9.80 and erased the 9.86 set by the Mopar of Bob Riffle.

In 1974, the NHRA revised its rules in Modified and allowed car owners to open up the rear wheelwells and relocate the frame rails for larger tires. As far as Ferrara's

After Richie Zul helped Dennis with the Motion car in 1974, the pair decided to run twin cars in 1975. Dennis received two engines from Zul, but oddly they both broke aluminum rods shifting into third gear. McBetts took over from there and built a healthy 432 with Carrillo rods that lasted the remainder of the season. (Photo Courtesy Todd Wingerter)

The Camaro doesn't look bad here before Dennis put it on a "performance enhancing weight loss program." Dennis stated his toughest competitor was John Lingenfelter and his Ford-powered Chevy Monza. "All that time I was struggling to beat John, [and] I come to find out he was using an illegal lock-up converter!" (Photo Courtesy Michael Pottie)

Proving that lighter is always better, Ferrara's Camaro went on a crash diet during 1977. A world title win in 1977 came on the back of national event wins at the Gatornationals, Sportsnationals, and World Finals. Division 1 points championships came in 1977 through 1980. (Photo Courtesy Michael Pottie)

Ferrara's World Championship–winning 379-ci engine was derived by destroking a 454 using a 348 crankshaft. Stock heads and a single 4-barrel carburetor were class requirements. Dennis ran a 9.39 to win the World Finals here at Ontario in 1977. (Photo Courtesy Bob Snyder)

Modified Eliminator's Electric Atmosphere

The sights and sounds of Modified Eliminator: 10,000-rpm launches, wheels high in the air, and the front end lurching wildly with each gear change. It was a time when the second-generation Corvette seemed to own Modified Eliminator. From Bob Callaham's evolutionary 1964 to Billy Mansel, whose 1965 holds the honor of being the last Corvette to win a Modified Eliminator crown, the Corvette is in the books as the winningest car in the category's history.

Tom Turner and his Modified Eliminator 1965 Corvette were Division 6 champs in 1976. The Corvette was reported to be the first D/MP car to run a 9-second time and set the class record with a 9.98 in August 1976. Caught here in action at Seattle in 1978, Tom played runner-up at the NHRA Winternationals and held the class record with an impressive 9.81. (Photo Courtesy Larry Pfister)

Before he hooked up with Reher-Morrison in 1985, Bruce Allen established himself running a Modified 1967 Camaro and this 1964 Corvette. Bruce's first ride with Reher-Morrison was at the NHRA Springnationals. He won three national events in 1985 and was runner-up at four more. This photo was taken at the 1979 Winternationals during class action. (Photo Courtesy Larry Pfister)

I don't think I could have picked a better example of the Corvettes that dominated Modified in the 1970s than Tony Christian's 1967 model. A racer since 1964, Tony's best year came in 1976 behind the wheel of this former Reher-Morrison car. Running 10.20 G/Gas times, Tony won three national events that year and had two runner-up finishes. The Pat Sullivan 287-ci engine definitely made power. (Photo Courtesy Mike Cochran)

Indiana's Albert Clark and Dave Coonce ran a long line of successful Modified and Comp Chevys. Big wins came at the U.S. Nationals in 1977 and 1979 in this Modified Corvette. A 287-ci and a Nash 5-speed propelled the Corvette to consistent 9.90s at over 130 mph. When the NHRA killed the category, the pair moved into Pro Stock. (Photo Courtesy Bob Martin)

Jerry Ault and Jim Derringer sure put the miles on this split-window Corvette. Seen here in 1975 running H/G with an injected 292-ci, the Ohio-based car held class records and was a class winner all the way back to its debut in 1972. A countless number of competitors benefited from a visit to Ault & James Speed Shop in Dayton, Ohio. As of this writing, Jerry is still building speed. (Photo Courtesy Bill Truby)

Martinez & Barth won the Gators and Indy in 1975, set the F/G record in August the same year, and held it through December 1976 at a best of 9.94 at 136.36 mph. The 1965 Corvette was the first 10 pounds per cubic inch car to run in the 9s. The 302-ci car started out in Modified before it moved to Gas in 1977. When Modified Eliminator was done away with, the Corvette moved into Altered. (Photo Courtesy Bill Truby)

The Vega that should have worked but didn't was purchased from an Alcohol racer. The 117-inch wheelbase was shortened to 107 in an attempt to repeat its 8.80 Winternationals times. Dennis eventually added weight to the car and ran it in B/EA before moving on. (Photo Courtesy Bob Boudreau)

Camaro was concerned, the mods proved to be just what the doctor ordered.

Now with yellow paint, the Camaro once again dropped the A/MP record and recorded a 9.54 at 145.16 mph in May. Dennis set it once again in November with a 9.39 and it stood until June 1977. Dennis recalled, "Although we owned the class, the car was heavy and broke a lot of parts. Rosen received an offer on the car that he just couldn't refuse, and off to Hawaii it went."

Dennis followed up with a 1969 Camaro for which Rosen paid the bills and sponsored. Dennis readily admitted it was a better car than the second-generation Camaro. "SRD put a chassis in it and floating rear." With a Richie Zul 427, the car ran 9.20s in A/MP. Dennis didn't care much for the 4-speed cars, as they were "parts breakers." In 1976, he pulled the engine and briefly ran it in an A/ED, recording 7.80 times.

Not a fan of running that quick, Dennis purchased the former *Grumpy's Toy*, a 1970½ Camaro from Richie Zul. Built to run B/EA, the car was thrown together, and untested, it immediately ran 9.60s with a McBetts 427 and won Comp at the Gatornationals.

Dennis introduced the world of drag racing to the trans brake, a device he developed with help from Roger Lamb. The brake that held the car in gear while Dennis brought the revs up was activated by an air solenoid that ran off a bottle of compressed air and consisted of a band around a drum off the back of the transmission. Dennis first ran the brake when he won the 1977 Sportsnationals and picked up a tenth of a second in the process.

With John Lingenfelter wreaking havoc through Econo Altered with his Ford-powered Monza, turning 9.20s and 9.30s, Dennis decided to shrink his big-block. As rules dictated stock heads, Dennis reasoned that you were basically enlarging the head by making the engine smaller.

"We went from 432 ci to 409. We also had a 393, which we ran most of the [1977] season. With the shorter-stroke motors, the powerband went up and up. We took a lot of weight out of the car. Going with a lighter fiberglass front end, we removed the inner fenders, added fiberglass doors with no windows, and ran a plexiglass windshield."

By the Fallnationals at Seattle, the Camaro ran a best of 9.31. At the 1977 NHRA World Finals, Dennis swapped out the tired 393 with a new 373 big-block.

"We were butting heads with Lingenfelter still and he was running 9.50s at the World Finals. We ran a 9.40 with the 373 and people screamed, figuring there was no way we could run that quick with an aluminum head." When Dennis defeated the Ford-powered E/A of Joe Williamson in the final, both Joe and Lingenfelter protested the Camaro. Dennis credited the win to the aluminum heads provided by Grumpy Jenkins. The heads carried a Chevy part number and were initially approved by the NHRA, but after the win Ferrara was told not to come back with them.

The same engine but with steel heads was run at the Little Guy Nationals, where it set the record running 9.35s. It drove Lingenfelter nuts because he still couldn't get out of the 9.40s with his Ford. Dennis eventually sold the car "to some street racers in Brooklyn because the NHRA killed the index. We put a bigger-inch motor in it and it still ran 9s."

Dennis made the move into A/EA with a short wheel-base Vega Funny Car that he referred to as a total disaster. "The car never worked right. I don't know why. We put the 373 engine from the Camaro in it and qualified number 1 at the Winternationals in 1978 but lost in the semifinals to Wayne Clapp." Dennis added some weight to the car, put it into B/EA, and ran 9.30s. He won Division 1 with the car but never won a national event.

"I hated the car. It was just rough and never ran 8s again after the Winternationals. We put the same motor in a Don Hardy Monza borrowed from Rick DeLisi [Waco Kid #1] and went a 9.0 to win the Winternationals." Dennis backed it up with wins at the Summernationals and the 1980 Gatornationals. "[At the Summernationals] I had three motors and three sets of heads and the NHRA

decided they didn't like any of my heads. They said they were worn-out used heads and I needed new castings. New heads went on with enough time for one qualifying attempt. We qualified number one and defeated Dempsey Hardy in the twin Waco car in the final."

The NHRA killed the index at the end of the season and the Monza was returned to DeLisi. Dennis followed with a brief stint in A/ED. He built a B/EA around 1981–1982 and used the former Waco Kid #2 Monza, an SRD car Dennis purchased that never ran as expected with the 373. He blew it up one day at West Hampton and put in a de-stroked big-block (using a 265 crankshaft and sleeved block) that measured 351 inches. He figured it would never run (high and narrow powerband), but it ran an 8.88, whereas the 373 was stuck in the 9.20s and 30s.

In total, Dennis won the Division 1 crown three times and won a world championship and seven national events before he sold the Monza to Mike Magistro and retired to the world of power boats.

Dennis Ferrara's A/ED ran a best of 7.82 at 171.95 mph in 1976, 0.23 under the class index. Showing just how successful the 409-ci rail was, many times it was the only dragster to qualify in Comp Eliminator. (Photo Courtesy Michael Pottie)

Bill Hielscher

Bill Hielscher, widely known as Mr. Bardahl, drove nothing but Chevys and is recognized as AHRA's winningest driver. Though his career as a traveling pro was a brief one and lasted less than 7 years, he managed to win 37 national events with 9 of them in a single season. With his Corvette and string of Camaros, he set more than 100 class records, was crowned AHRA World Champion seven times, and accomplished the feat in two categories one year. This feat has never been accomplished by anyone in any sanctioning body.

Born in Indiana, Bill relocated to Texas and became serious about drag racing around 1962. He paid his dues in Stock, running his *Lucky 7* '57 Chevy before he turned pro with his much ballyhooed small-block powered 1965 Corvette. The car debuted in 1966 and Bill won 9 of 10 AHRA national events. The Corvette proved to be the consummate AHRA formula car. With a simple switch in engines or even swapping out the intake and carb, the Corvette could and would dominate a number of classes.

Not content to own AHRA Super Stock, GT, and the Street categories, Hielscher hauled a pair of his drag cars

It's unlikely that there was a harder-working person in drag racing than Bill Hielscher. Along with running a fleet of drag cars, a racetrack, and conducting sponsor clinics, he ran a successful machine shop/ speed shop in Irving, Texas. This black and white photo doesn't do the colorful Corvette justice. (Photo Courtesy Edelbrock LLC Archives)

Bill's 1968 lineup included two Corvettes, two Camaros, and a speed boat? Yup, it's rat-powered. The Bardahl company continues to sponsor all forms of motorsport. Ole Bardahl loved his speed boats. The Miss Bardahl *hydroplane was a six-time National Champion and five-time Gold Cup winner that raced from 1957 to 1969. Jones and Gotcher ran the 1968 Camaro on the left and worked as salesmen at Friendly Chevrolet. (Photo Courtesy Edelbrock LLC Archives)*

It's not a clinic—more like a traveling road show. There were few better PR men for the sport and the sponsors than Bill Hielscher. The Camaro on the trailer is Bill's 302-powered GT-3 car. (Photo Courtesy Michael Pottie)

to Bonneville in 1969. That was a trip that he repeated in 1970, netting himself two land speed records. In B/GT, his 327-powered Corvette ran 170.69 mph, while his 427-powered 1968 Camaro cranked a 188.75 mph to earn the title of the world's fastest carbureted production car. Bill proved to be one of the hardest-working men in drag racing; by 1971, there were nine cars running under the Mr. Bardahl umbrella. Always the promoter, part of Bill's traveling show was sponsor displays and a clinic program.

Hielscher was the first Chevy racer to debut a second-gen Camaro Pro Stocker and did so at the NHRA Gatornationals in 1970. Bill failed to qualify his seven-day wonder, and like all second-generation Camaros facing the hemi onslaught, the car had a tough time putting wins together. Hielscher's final year on the road was 1972, and true to form, he went out on top. Using his trusted Corvette, the same car that launched his career, Bill won Super Stock Eliminator at the AHRA Grand American race in Tulsa, Oklahoma. Bill never raced again and is said to be the only professional drag racer to end his career with a national event win.

Out from behind the wheel, Bill busied himself as owner and operator of Green Valley Raceway. He returned to racing in 1977 as a team leader of seven cars.

The yellow and black paint combo, dreamed up by Bill because he felt it would be noticeable and not because it was Bardahl colors, remained. He manned Green Valley until it closed in 1986.

Dave Jones drove Bill Heilscher's 1968 Camaro in GT-2 and won the championship with it in 1970, losing only 2 of the season's 10 races. Times of 11.40s were the norm for the big-block-powered car. (Photo Courtesy Michael Pottie)

Bo started racing with a Modified Production '57 Chevy that was equipped with a tunnel-rammed 327. Here his Corvette is caught in action at the World Finals in 1969. The car could run a half-second under its 11.34 record. Bo states that the black and gold colors were inspired by Smokey Yunick. (Photo Courtesy Steve Reyes)

Harold "Bo" Laws

Bo Laws's machine and parts company of Orlando, Florida, was responsible for building some pretty potent cars during the latter half of the 1960s and into the 1970s; none more so than the 1967 Corvette of Bruce Behrens. The car won a couple national events and held records in two different classes for two years prior to the NHRA killing off the Sports Production category at the end of 1969.

Bruce purchased the Goodwood Green Corvette new with the idea of going road racing. Bruce had never tried his hand on a road course, so with a little coaxing from Bo, he decided drag racing would be the better choice. Bo began preparing the car late in 1967. He used the best available factory parts in the 390-hp 427 and complemented them with goods from Manley, Sig Erson, and Edelbrock. The 427 was backed with a Muncie 4-speed stuffed with bulletproof BorgWarner gears. Not satisfied with the Muncie offerings of a 2.20 or 2.54 first gears, Bo used his connections at BorgWarner to secure a 2.43 first, 1.77 second, and 1.23 third. Bo felt the gears were worth a good tenth of a second.

As most know, the weak link in these Corvettes is the independent rear suspension. Bo discovered his one-ton truck U-joints were failing because of the way the car squatted coming off the line. "This put side pressure on the needle bearings, causing them to fail, so we did two things. We took out the needle bearings and made brass bushings. Second, we removed the clips that retained the axles, which allowed them to slide out about a quarter inch each time we accelerated." The posi unit was a different story, and Bo could do little about breakage except carry a spare. To make the removal and replacement eas-

ier, Bo cut an access hole in the floorboard. Two people could swap out the third member in 25 minutes.

Though Bruce Behrens owned the Corvette, the decision was made early on that Bo would do the driving. They completed the car shortly before the NHRA Winternationals, and Bo had just one outing in it before Bruce

> **"It was tough, tough competition, and you really had to fight to win."**
> **– Harold "Bo" Laws**

decided he wanted to haul it out to Pomona for the 1968 Winter meet. In D/SP, Bo cleared class with a 12.29 before he sailed through Street Eliminator and defeated the Chevy-powered C/Gas Anglia of Bob Riffle in the final round. Three months later, Bo set both C and D/SP class records at Phenix City with clockings of 11.34 at 125.00 mph and 11.61 at 121.13 mph.

He followed with a win of Modified Eliminator at the NHRA Springnationals and defeated the Corvette of Jim Elliot in the final. He failed to make it a three-peat at Indy when he broke the rear end and had no time to repair it.

Bruce sold the Corvette to Bo at the end of the season, as Bruce's thoughts once more turned to road racing. Bo ran the Corvette through 1969, when he won the Division 2 crown and played runner-up to Mike Fons at the World Finals. Life was getting busy for Bo as he split his time between the track, a growing family, and his business. To lighten the load, partner Fred Kinney was behind the wheel on alternate weekends.

In 1970, Bo built a 1969 Camaro and gave the world of Pro Stock a try, but not before entertaining an offer from Chrysler to run a Superbird in Super Stock. Bo shot them down, as he had no interest in running slower in a bigger car. Though he saw most of his success behind the wheel of the Corvette, the Pro Stock Camaros are what Bo is most proud of. "It was tough, tough competition, and you really had to fight to win."

Though national event wins escaped him, Bo did pretty good in division races. A staging lane accident at Indy saw Bob Banning's Plymouth rear-end Bo's Camaro and all but destroy the car and send Bo to the hospital with a broken back. He recovered and returned with a second Camaro to start the 1971 season. A 427 4-speed Dana combo delivered 9.70 times before Bo retired from active racing at the end of the season.

There was a total of seven cars that ran under the Bo Laws umbrella, one being Roger Vinci's gorgeous D/Altered '55. Roger took over Bo Laws Automotive in 1968 when Bo opened his machine and parts business. His '55 was powered by a Hilborn-injected 302 4-speed and Pontiac rear. The '55 ran a best of 10.77 at 127 mph. (Author's Collection)

Bo debuted his second Camaro Pro Stocker, seen here at Indy against Dave Strickler, in January 1971. He won his share of division races and still gets a kick out of having beaten Sox & Martin at Hollywood, Florida. Though tough to make out here, the license plate reads "Chrysler Test Car." (Photo Courtesy Steve Reyes)

The summer of 1972 was a good one for Larry Nelson. In a two-week period that included the Summernationals, Larry saw the '55 pay for itself by winning a total of $8,500. He beat Bob Glidden twice at Kil-Kare before winning at Bowling Green and Englishtown. At the World Finals, Larry collected another $3,500 when he played runner-up in the final to Dave Boertman. (Photo Courtesy Bob Martin)

Larry Nelson

Ohio resident Larry Nelson was another fan favorite who left an impression in Super Modified, Stock, Comp, and, well, you get the picture. Larry seemed to come out of nowhere in 1972 to win the NHRA Summernationals with his SS/T '55 Chevy business coupe. It was a car built with partner Duane Brock, and the Summernationals was the first national event either had ever entered.

In the final, Larry defeated the SS/Q 1965 Chevelle wagon of Tony Cieri. In the process, Larry dropped the class record from 13.40 to 13.20. He backed up his Sum-

Larry said, "We actually bought a two-door and four-door wagon to run different classes. We'd swap the engine, 3-speed, and 12-bolt from the sedan into the wagon." The wagon took SS/U at the U.S. Nationals in 1973 with mid-13 times. (Photo Courtesy Larry Nelson)

mernationals win the following week at National Trail, where he won the National Dragster Open. At the NHRA World Final in Amarillo, Nelson qualified number 2 and battled his way to the final round, where he fell to the factory-backed Mopar of Dave Boertman. In trying to hold off the charge of Boertman, Larry lowered the class record once again, this time to a 13.06 at 105.28 mph. Brock and Nelson alternated between the sedan and a wagon through 1973 and swapped the 265 3-speed transmission and 12-bolt rear end back and forth between the two so they could compete in alternate classes.

Shortly after the World Finals, Larry landed a cushy job at Jegs Automotive, now called Jegs High Performance. In 1974, Larry approached the boss, Jeg Coughlin Sr., about sponsoring a Super Stock Chevelle he was considering building. "He had an empty garage beside the apartment I was renting, and I wanted it to build my Chevelle, so I said I'd put his name on the car for the use of the garage. A couple days later he called me back into his office and asked me to consider running this new class that was in the works: A/Super Modified." Larry was made an offer he couldn't refuse and he jumped at the opportunity. The Chevelle was forgotten, and in its place a Super Modified–friendly Chevy II was purchased.

A/SM class rules dictated that the car had to be 1967 or newer, so Larry hunted down a well-worn sedan and he and his partner, Mark Williams, set to work. Why a Chevy II as opposed to the oh-so-popular first-gen Camaro? Well, being limited to a 10.5-inch tire (another rule), Larry reasoned that the Chevy II's extra foot of rear

The NHRA added two more classes to Super Modified in 1976. With a small-inch mouse under the hood, the Chevy II moved into C/SM and recorded 10.70 times. Ladder bars and 10.5-Goodyears made for a great launch. (Photo Courtesy Larry Nelson)

Larry Nelson, in the far lane, stuck with Chevy after moving into Super Comp in the Jegs-sponsored rear-engine car. A 355 propelled the car to a couple major event wins. (Photo Courtesy Larry Nelson)

Super Modified debuted at the U.S. Nationals in 1975 and was dominated by Camaros and Chevy IIs. Larry Nelson waded through them all to come out as class winner running a 10.82. (Photo Courtesy Dan Williams)

Scott Shafiroff's History with Chevys

Though Scott Shafiroff turned to running a (gulp) Ford in 1975, he still deserves a mention for the killer Chevys he ran before and after. Those of us old enough have fond memories of his 1968 Camaro that dominated IHRA's SS-2 class and the AHRA GT-2 and GT-3 in 1972. Running Truppi-Kling single 4-barrel engines that ranged in size from 302 to 327 ci, the record-holding car was capable of 10.30 times. On his website, shafiroff.com, Scott recounted how they were competitive right off the bat. "In 1972, we just dominated AHRA and IHRA, winning 9 out of 13 races and playing runner-up at two more."

In AHRA competition, Scott earned a phenomenal 7,000 points, which was second only to Don Garlits. The feat earned Scott AHRA's Sportsman Driver of the Year honors. The AHRA dropped the GT category at the end of 1972, and the IHRA did the same with the Super Stock category the next year. Both moves were due to the domination of Chevys run by Scott, the Kimball brothers, Hielscher, and others.

The "Kid From New York City" moved on to Pro Stock in 1973 with an SRD Vega. Using Truppi-Kling small-blocks for power, the car won numerous match races and made a few AHRA final-round appearances. After a bout with a Pro Stock Mustang II, Scott returned to Chevy in 1981 with a Super Pro Monza. Powered by a single 4-barrel big-inch big-block on nitrous, the Powerglide-equipped car was capable of 7.80 times, which was at least 3/10 quicker than his nearest competition. In 1983, he teamed with driver Gordy Hmiel to run a Pro Mod Camaro. Aptly named the Over the Hill Gang, the seemingly ageless Scott proved anything but. Today, Shafiroff Racing builds some of the most potent engines in the country.

Car Craft *magazine called this the car that killed the AHRA GT classes. By the time the category was dropped in 1972, the only competitive cars were first-generation Camaros from the Kimball brothers, Gene Dunlap, Hielscher, et al. (Photo Courtesy Bob Martin)*

Scott Shafiroff and his SRD Vega were heavy-hitters with Truppi-Kling power. Scott quickly learned to make power on his own, and today his business building potent Chevy engines thrives. (Photo Courtesy Todd Wingerter)

Larry's T-1000 made use of a Super Duty iron block and an aluminum head that was ported and carried titanium valves and Jesel rockers. The engine featured lots of compression and buzzed to 10,000 rpm. Larry ran the car most of the time with an automatic transmission. (Photo Courtesy Larry Nelson)

overhang would aid traction. In hindsight, he said they probably should have gone with a hardtop because he found out later that they have a lower silhouette. The Chevy II went together over the winter of 1974–1975 with power from a punched-out 327 measuring 331 inches. Completing the driveline was a 2.64 first gear Super T-10 and Dana 60 rear end. Roger Burkett at Jegs helped with the build by narrowing the chassis, stretching the wheelwells, and tying the frame. At the 1975 Winternationals, Larry drove the car to a class win at the inaugural Super Modified race.

The category was expanded two more classes in its second year, and a new engine moved the Chevy II down to C/SM. A 0.030-over 283 that measured 288 ci was built and filled with Arias pistons, Superrod aluminum rods, and a Crane 0.669-lift cam. By 1977, Racing Head Services was giving the team free cylinder heads. Rules limited head mods to one inch under the valve seat and 1 inch into the ports. Compression squeezed out to 13:1. A Holley 750 set atop an Edelbrock Scorpion II intake. Spent gases were expelled through Hooker headers. A Schiefer clutch sat in front of the Super T-10 that now carried a 2.80 first gear. The 6.17-geared Dana was supported by mono-leaf springs and Competition Engineering ladder bars.

The Chevy II was the first Super Modified car to make it to a national event final, doing so at the 1977 Sportsnationals. In the final, Larry fell to the B/Street Roadster of Dave Hutchens and turned a 10.71 at 124.32 mph.

Larry gathered his share of class wins and bracket raced the heck out of the car before the NHRA killed Modified Eliminator in 1981. He ran the Chevy II briefly in 1982 as a Super Stocker before he took a break from the sport. The Chevy II was sold to Bob Fordyce and campaigned on the West Coast before it was sold to a racer in New Zealand.

Larry returned in 1983 with a small-block-powered Super Comp rail that knocked off 8.80 times to win the Sportsnationals and the *Popular Hot Rodding* meet. Larry followed up with a 165-ci Iron Duke–powered SS/GC Pontiac T-1000. He squeezed 11-second times from the car before he retired in 2006. After 20 years of racing, it was quite the run. The '55 sedan that started it all is back in Larry's hands and is being prepared to once again take on the world of Super Stock.

Larry Kopp

Journalist Rick Voegelin wrote a great piece on Larry Kopp where he referred to the man as "the uncrowned king of NHRA Modified Eliminator," and rightly so. Larry was the most successful racer in the category's 12-year history (1970–1981) and won a total of nine national events. In 1976, he won the world championship.

Larry grew up in Baltimore, Maryland, during the 1960s and had a passion for cars. He graduated from Overlea High in 1966 and went to work for his dad at Ted's Towing Service, a company Larry later operated. Like many of us, Larry started out street racing before he graduated to run regularly at his home track of Cecil County with a 409-powered Biscayne. He first caught national attention while running a 302-powered '57 Chevy wagon in Modified Eliminator. The *Mad-Man* wagon briefly held the F/G class ET record in 1972 with an 11.58.

Larry captured his first national event win in 1976 when he won the World Finals behind the wheel of his H/G 1964 Corvette. In the final round, Larry recorded a 10.84 at 106 mph to defeat Tony Christian in the former Reher-Morrison G/Gas Corvette. Larry ran his Corvette through 1976 and held multiple class records over the period. He returned in 1977 and wore the number 1 on a 1961 Corvette. Like his 1964, the new car was prepped by SRD Race Cars and featured a small-inch engine. He ran the Corvette in D and E/MP through 1978 and picked up three more national event wins and a few runner-up finishes. The car was a consistent record holder and ran times in the 9.80s at more than 136 mph.

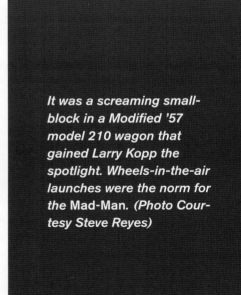

It was a screaming small-block in a Modified '57 model 210 wagon that gained Larry Kopp the spotlight. Wheels-in-the-air launches were the norm for the Mad-Man. (Photo Courtesy Steve Reyes)

A change of direction in 1980 saw Larry debut an SRD-prepped B/MP Malibu. Though the lightweight Malibu with its Dave Alosio–built 323-ci looked good on paper, the car failed to meet Larry's expectations. Class wins and 9.40 times were realized before Larry moved on.

At the end of the season, he purchased the proven Dave Hutchens Wayne County Opel. Dave had won four Modified national events with the Mike Sullivan–built car before Larry went on a tear of his own with it. He won five national events in 1981 and played runner-up at

three more events, including two in Comp Eliminator. He finished the 1981 season third in points after a nail-biting World Final showdown.

As innovative as the Opel was, it wasn't without controversy. A trick clutchless 5-speed transmission, when clutchless transmissions were supposed to be illegal in Modified, really caught the ire of competitors.

When the NHRA did away with Modified Eliminator, Larry moved into Comp with a B/MP third-generation Camaro. He followed with an Olds Cutlass

Don't let the nondescript plain white paint on Larry Kopp's 1964 Corvette fool you. Between 1974 and 1976, the car put the hurt on many Gas and Modified Production competitors. Larry ran small-blocks down to 287 ci in the SRD-prepped car and recorded a 10.29 to win C/MP at Indy in 1976. The car was a multiple class record holder through 1976. In 1977, Modified Production wheelbase rules were set at a 97-inch minimum to make the car illegal. (Photo Courtesy Michael Pottie)

Kopp's Corvette wore the number 1 after winning the Modified Championship in 1976. Running E/MP, Kopp won the Fallnationals and Summernationals in 1977 and won his third straight division title. He repeated the victory at Fallnationals in 1978. With a 288-ci engine for power, the car recorded high-9s at 136 mph. (Photo Courtesy Michael Pottie)

in the 1990s before he moved into Pro Stock Truck in 1998. With a Grumpy Jenkins 358 under the hood, Larry captured the World Championship that inaugural year on the strength of 7.60 times and four national event wins. The first time out for Kopp in the S-10 was at the Fram Route 66 Springnationals at Dallas, where

he took the win and set the mile per hour record at the same time.

Larry was a well-liked guy with a career that was the envy of many. He returned to Comp Eliminator when the Pro Stock Truck category was eliminated and raced until his untimely passing in 2004.

Built by Mike Sullivan and initially driven by Dave Hutchens under the Wayne County banner, this Opel more than pushed the envelope. Between 1979 and 1987, the car was campaigned by Hutchens, Kopp, and Todd Patterson. Between Modified and Comp, the Opel won 11 NHRA national events and a world title in 1980. All with Chevy power, of course. (Photo Courtesy Dave Kommel)

Ken Veney's Vegas

Ken Veney is nothing short of a mechanical genius. Success, be it with Chevys, his own-design hemi heads, Funny Cars, or Tractor Pullers, has followed him wherever he goes. He began his reign of terror in BB/FC during 1972 with an injected big-block Chevy Vega. In 1973, he added nitro to the mix and set the A/FC record with a 7.45. The NHRA debuted Pro Comp at the 1973 season-ending Supernationals, and to no one's surprise, Veney qualified

number one and finished as runner-up. He made Pro Comp's first 6-second run, doing so at the 1974 Winternationals, where he played runner-up to Dale Armstrong's Veney-powered A/FD.

Ken had four Vegas in total: an injected Chevy on alcohol in 1972, a new injected nitro car in 1973, a blown alcohol car in 1974 (the 1973 car with a 1974 nose graft), and a Keith Black hemi-powered candy red car in 1975.

Night action is shown at Irwindale in 1973 when Ken Veney faced Dale Armstrong in an all-Veney Chevy Comp final. The pair met again in the final round of the World Finals in 1975 with Dale Armstrong coming out on top. (Photo Courtesy Steve Reyes)

☆☆☆ THE BEST OF THE REST ☆☆☆

Competition was the toughest in the Sportsman categories as pretty much anything was allowed: big-blocks, small-blocks, Hemis, and Cammers in everything from dragsters, gassers, altereds, door cars, and Econo Funny Cars—any combination you could imagine. The winning racers had choices, and they chose wisely.

Between the years 1964 and 1968, few Gassers were as feared as Ray and Ed Kohler's 1951 Anglia. King Kong was the brothers' first venture into the world of drag racing, and boy did they build a winner. In 1965, it took A/G at both the NHRA and AHRA Winter meets, and followed up with a class win at the Smokers Meet at Bakersfield. Initially they ran a 388-inch Chevy and later switched to a bored and stroked big-block that measured 454 inches. Record-setting times in the 9.20s were the norm. (Photo Courtesy Lou Hart)

Skip Hess and partner Jim "Fireball" Shores' 1949 Anglia was one of the first to run a big-block Chevy. Also, they have been credited with coining the term "rat motor" in reference to the new Chevy mill. The pair debuted their Don Long–built Anglia in 1965 with a 375-inch small-block Chevy and promptly set the class speed record at 137.40 mph. By the end of the season, the Anglia sported the rat motor and competed strongly in AHRA A/GS competition. (Author's Collection)

Well into the 1970s, The Street Cleaner roadster of Jerry Hays was one of the fiercest in the nation. Jerry initially ran a Gene Adams–built Olds in the 1928 Ford that earned him A/SR honors at the 1964 NHRA Winternationals. By 1966, a 427 Chevy filled the rails and helped Jerry earn wins at both the AHRA and NHRA Winternationals, as well as Bakersfield and the Hot Rod magazine meet. A Hemi was tried before upkeep saw Jerry return the roadster to Chevy power. (Photo Courtesy Steve Reyes)

The Jewel T was campaigned in 1967–1968 by Joe Davis, Wes Ingram, and Jim Walvern. Joe drove the 427-powered T to a total of seven class records. Topping the team's accomplishments was winning the 1967 NHRA Super Eliminator title. The T was credited with a number of firsts, including the first Altered to run in the 7s on gas. (Photo Courtesy James Handy)

Jack Ditmars was dominant in the Altered ranks during the mid-1960s with his small-block-powered 1934 Ford. With a 30-percent shot of nitro, the Lil Screamer II was capable of low 9-second times at 150 mph. Between 1963 and the time he sold the car in 1967, Ditmars captured something like a dozen class wins at national events. (Photo Courtesy Michael Pottie)

George "Buddy" Owens won the 1971 Gatornationals and Springnationals in E/MP. His Nova made a lot of trips down the track and is seen here at the 1979 Winternationals, where it ran C/SM. Buddy is another who still builds competitive engines. (Photo Courtesy Dave Kommel)

☆ ☆ ☆ THE BEST OF THE REST ☆ ☆ ☆

Pete Bergen and Wayne Burrows's gorgeous D/A '56 Corvette had no problem getting the wheels up thanks to a Kinsler-injected 288-ci engine and a 2.64 low-gear T10 transmission behind a 60-pound flywheel. A 1959 Pontiac rear end with 6.14 gears ensured few beat it off the line. The 'glass wonder based in Allenwood, Pennsylvania, ran bottom 11s at high 120s as the 1960s drew to a close. (Photo Courtesy Michael Pottie)

Washington's Frizzel brothers' Camaro (they had two) ran small-blocks that measured anywhere from 292 to 331 inches. Driver Carl Frizzel launched the car at 10,500 rpm and recorded mid-10-second times. A Doug Nash 5-speed and Ford rear end completed the bulletproof drivetrain that helped the brothers earn numerous class wins and records. (Photo Courtesy Larry Pfister)

Paul Sable's gorgeous F/MP 1954 Chevy really stood out in a category stacked with Camaros and Corvettes. Motivation for the 3,370-pound car came by way of a Tony Feil 287-ci engine backed by a Muncie M-22 and an Olds rear with 5.13 gears. Believing Chevrolet is the only way, this was Paul's first car that he purchased back in 1961 when he was 16. It was a daily driver until he went drag racing with it around 1964. He still owns the car. (Photo Courtesy Bob Boudreau)

Dave Lewis built the Granny Goose to compete in D/MP with a 0.030-over 302. He debuted the Camaro on Easter Sunday in 1971 and earned the class record shortly after with an 11.11. The gorgeous multihued paint was courtesy of Bill Roell and Jim "Dauber" Farr. Jerry Coley bought the Camaro in 1974 and won class at both the Winternationals and Gatornationals. He closed out the season by taking the Division 2 modified crown. (Photo Courtesy Bob Martin)

One part of Sam Gianino's flamed four-car team in 1972 was the D/Gas Camaro of Al Maynard. Al's 1967 Camaro, formerly owned by Mike Fons, ran a stroked 330-incher with Kinsler injectors. A Doug Nash–prepped BorgWarner and 6.17 rear gears rounded out the drivetrain. Times of 10.60s at close to 130 mph were the norm. (Photo Courtesy Michael Cochran)

★★☆ *THE BEST OF THE REST* ☆★★

Out of Omaha rolled Charlie Jacobs and Rich Mlnarik's hot little E/MP Camaro. The car featured a Ford 9-inch rear, a Nash transmission, and Jacobs-built small-blocks in sizes 287, 292, and 296 ci. Later motors were based upon a de-stroked 350. In 1973, Charlie won the Popular Hot Rodding race and set the E/MP record at 11.08. The Camaro ran a best of 10.80 at 128 mph before it was replaced with a Super Modified Chevy II. (Photo Courtesy Tommy Shaw)

Wayne and Dan Jesel, with partner Terry Clark, ran this SRD 1974 Camaro in both D/Altered and C/FX through 1977. Wayne manned the controls and Dan built the 302. A 4-speed Lenco was used until the NHRA outlawed it. The guys then switched to a clutchless Doug Nash 4+1. Wayne said, "We were Doug's test car for it. The car was a multiple-class winner and record holder; a lot of fun." (Photo Courtesy Bob Boudreau)

Doc Dixon ran the gambit of drag cars but had his most success behind the wheel of the 1969 Camaro. A tunnel-rammed small-block, 4-speed, and Dana rear produced record 10.50 times. The Sherrodsville, Ohio, resident used the combo to win the 1974 Modified Eliminator World Championship. (Photo Courtesy Bill Truby)

Harry Luzader first entered the record books back in 1966 with an unforgettable Chevy-powered D/G 1932 Ford. He debuted his Opel in 1970 and set records in E and F/Gas. In 1976, the 280-plus cubic incher held the E/G mark with a 9.89 at 138.46 mph. In total, Harry grabbed class 17 times at national events and won the Division 1 title four years running—all with Chevy power. (Photo Courtesy Bob Martin)

Gene Dunlap, in the former Hiner-Miller Camaro, ran SS-2 in 1972 with a 331-ci Chrysler 4-speed and Dana rear end. Between 1970 and 1972, Gene won himself a "couple handfuls of AHRA and IHRA events," recording 10.90 times. Here at Tennessee, Gene is facing his partner Gary Perdew. (Photo Courtesy Steve Reyes)

Hielscher focused his attention on AHRA tracks and rarely ran NHRA races. Here he's running his 427 Camaro heads-up Super Stock in 1970 against Arlen Vanke at the AHRA Winternationals held at Bee Line in Arizona. (Photo Courtesy Michael Pottie)

Chapter Five

Pro Stock Brigade

Pro Stock is everyone's favorite category, or at least it was at one time. Born out of heads-up, run-whatcha-brung match racing, the UDRA was the first to run a class legal heads-up program in 1967. The AHRA followed suit in 1968, the NHRA joined the party in 1970, and the IHRA followed in 1971. Beyond safety requirements, rules were minimal and the focus was on specific weight requirements, cubic-inch limits, and tire size. It was a see-saw battle throughout the decade as Chevy, Ford, and Mopar each showed dominance at different times. Chevy garnered 22 NHRA national event wins through the decade with the Camaro doing the most damage.

The Kimball Brothers

The AHRA was the first to crown a world champion when it implemented a points collection program in 1969. At the end of the season, Missouri residents Gary and Larry Kimball had collected 30,000 points with their Camaro to earn the title. The Kimballs had been kicking around drag racing for a few years; Gary ran a 1965 Mustang with friend John Hill while Larry teamed with a gentleman by the name of Duey Adams and ran a big-block-powered 1965 Chevelle. It was John Hill, a wealthy Missouri farmer, who suggested they join forces and buy Grumpy Jenkins's 1967 Camaro that had just come up for sale. The Kimballs knew a winner when they saw one and jumped at the opportunity. John laid out the long green for the car and a little extra for one Jenkins-prepped 427. Gary took on the driving chores and went on a holy tear with the car and won nearly every event he entered.

Gary continued to run AHRA Pro Stock (heads-up S/S) with the Camaro until the brothers debuted their Pro Stock Vega in the spring of 1971. The Camaro was then converted to run AHRA's GT-2. Introduced in 1970 as a

The Kimball brothers took Grumpy Jenkins's old toy and made it an AHRA World Champion in 1969. Here, Larry faces the 1968 Camaro of Wally Booth. Both cars were 427-powered. The Kimballs' Camaro had a best time of 9.84 at 138.84 mph. (Photo Courtesy Michael Pottie)

The Kimballs were a dominating force in the AHRA GT classes and won GT-1 its opening season. Times of 10.90s were common for this Junior Pro Stocker driven by Larry in 1971. Three heads-up Grand Touring (GT) classes were introduced in 1970 and allowed for 1967 or newer cars. Each class was based upon the following cubic-inch-per-pound break: GT-1 was for cars with 401 or greater ci that weighed in at a minimum 8 pounds per cubic inch, GT-2 consisted of cars with 350- to 400-ci with a minimum 9 pounds per inch, and GT-3 was 300- to 349-ci cars at 10 pounds per inch. Initially rules called for a single 4-barrel and no tunnel rams. (Author's Collection)

sort of junior Pro Stock, there eventually were three GT classes that were all run in the heads-up format. Simultaneous to running GT-2, Gary ran a 1969 Camaro in GT-3. Larry meanwhile ran a second Camaro, a 1968 previously purchased from a local Kansas racer, in GT-1 with a ZL1.

The Kimballs' Vega was the first legal Pro Stock Vega on the scene and made its debut in the spring of 1971. Driven by Gary, the Don Hardy–built car competed in AHRA competition and initially ran mid-10s using a destroked Don Young 400 that measured 321 ci. A switch to a proven 302 netted bottom-10s for the new age Pro Stocker. It's interesting to note that at the same time Hardy was building the Kimballs' Vega, he had another Vega in the shop coming together for Gary's former partner, John Hill. Building the car to AHRA rules, John made use of a Booth-Arons 432-inch engine, Chrysler crash box, and Dana rear that propelled his Vega to early 10.30 times at 135 mph.

For the 1973 season, the brothers had Hardy tweak the suspension and add tubs to the rear of the Vega. By mid-summer, Grumpy Jenkins pieced together a 331-ci for them. Before the engine was completed though, trag-

edy struck. While attending a race at Springfield, Missouri, Gary was struck by a flying piece of debris while standing near the starting line. He succumbed to his injuries on September 15. Larry attempted to carry on

The Kimball brothers split driving chores with their 1969 Camaro. Gary drove it in AHRA GT-3 in 1970 and GT-2 in 1971. Larry ran the car in both AHRA and IHRA during 1972 and 1973. (Photo Courtesy Todd Wingerter)

The Kimballs' last kick at the can came in 1973 when they campaigned this Pro Stock Vega. Don Hardy was in the process of building a new Vega for the brothers when Gary was killed. That car was completed for Bruce Larson. Larry carried on briefly in this car with a hired driver, but a clash in personalities doomed it from the get-go. (Photo Courtesy Dennis Doubleday)

and briefly ran the Vega with a hired driver. Larry, a man with strong Christian beliefs, clashed with the hired gun, who, in contrast, spent much of his time looking into a bottle. Larry retired in 1973 and rarely spoke of the period between 1968 and 1973 when he and his brother dominated AHRA action.

Bill "Grumpy" Jenkins

The first-gen Camaro was the go-to car during the initial years of Pro Stock, and more often than not Bill Jenkins and his line of *Grumpy's Toys* led the charge. At the NHRA's inaugural Pro Stock race, the Winternationals, 49 percent of the entries were Chevys. In the category final, Jenkins, in his 1968 Camaro *Grumpy's Toy IV*, turned a 9.98 to defeat the 10.13 turned by Sox & Martin's 1970

'Cuda. Worth noting is the fact that Jenkins's Camaro was the only Pro Stocker to break the 10-second barrier that weekend. The Grump would make it two national event wins in a row when he defeated Ronnie Sox at the Gatornationals. To face the onslaught of Hemi Mopars and Cammer Fords, Jenkins relied upon an all-aluminum Can-Am 430-ci engine. This was an engine developed for USAC racing and featured a favorable 4.44-inch bore. It was a stronger block than the more common ZL1, but unless you were well connected with Chevrolet, there was no way you were going to get your hands on one.

Bill debuted his second-gen Camaro, *Grumpy's Toy VIII*, in the summer of 1970. By that point, the factory-backed Mopars had taken charge of Pro Stock. Jenkins's Camaro, like the other Chevys and the Fords, was little

Few Camaros are as recognizable as Grumpy's Toy IV. Bill first ran the car in S/S, then in Modified Production, and finally Pro Stock. The 430-powered car was the first Pro Stocker to run 9-second times. (Photo Courtesy Michael Pottie)

more than fodder for the Hemis through 1971. It seemed no matter what combo the Grump tried, the new car failed to meet with success. In legal trim, the Camaro ran no better than an on-the-record 9.52. In match race guise, it was a different story. Bill unleashed his Mountain Motor, a 494 cubic incher built using the aluminum Can-Am block, and defeated Don Nicholson and Ronnie Sox with a best of 9.26 ET during a match race in West Palm Beach, Florida.

The 1971 NHRA season closed with Chrysler cars winning all but one national event. Late in the season Jenkins met with NHRA Executive Vice President Jack Hart in hopes of hammering out some new rules that would level the playing field. Without new rules, Jenkins had plans to abandon NHRA Pro Stock and build a big-inch Vega match racer.

Jenkins proposed rules and weight breaks that would favor small cubic inch, short-wheelbase compact cars, such as the Chevy Vega and Ford Pinto. The small car idea was sold to Jack from a marketing perspective: The buying public was purchasing small cars, and by racing the same, the crowds would pour in.

The NHRA agreed and new rules were written for the 1972 season. Of course, Chrysler, the only factory putting money into drag racing, sensed its domination was coming to an end and protested the move to no avail. The weight breaks for the coming season saw wedge-engine cars carry 6.75 pounds per cubic inch; inclined-valve engines carried 7.0; and all others, specifically SOHC Fords and Chrysler Hemis, 7.25.

Jenkins and his Super Crew set to work building a 331-ci Vega. S-W Race Cars welded up a 360-degree, 4130 chrome-moly tube roll cage. The Vega was like no other Pro Stocker ever built. The tubing tied the stock front rails with a tube rear chassis. A narrowed 12-bolt rear and four-link suspension was attached. Jenkins debuted the Vega at the season-opening NHRA Winternationals and dominated the field with 9.60 times. He had the Mopars covered by almost two-tenths of a second, and in the final round, he defeated the Hemi 'Cuda of Don Grotheer. Jenkins owned the season and took the championship after winning six of seven national events he entered. Bill ran two more Vegas through 1974 and garnered additional national event wins.

The one constant in Pro Stock throughout the decade was the fluctuating weight breaks. Every year, and usually more than once a year, the NHRA made adjustments if it felt one brand showed dominance over the others. In almost everyone's book, it did a poor job. The breaks seemed to favor the Cleveland-powered Fords—between 1973 and 1981, they won all but one world title. In 1976, Jenkins bucked the odds when he won his second world championship of the decade. Using a wind-cheating, SRD-built Monza, Jenkins and driver Larry Lombardo won three national events and held off late charges by Warren Johnson and the AMC Hornet of Wally Booth. In AHRA competition where things were a little more balanced, driver Ken Dondero won a pair of world championships in Jenkins's second Monza. By this point of the decade, Jenkins's 331-ci mills were pulling 2 hp per cubic

The Grump and his evolutionary 1972 Vega were a definite game changer. A 0.030-over 327 running consistent 9.40s put the Hemis and Fords on the trailer. With five national event wins in 1972 and the world championship, you can be sure the Grump was all smiles. (Photo Courtesy Michael Pottie)

Larry Lombardo proved to be more than a capable hired gun and won the world title for Jenkins in 1976. In 1977, Jenkins and crew cleaned house at the Car Craft awards banquet and took Pro Stock crew chief, Pro Stock driver (Larry Lombardo), and Pro Stock engine builder (Joe Tryson). (Photo Courtesy Dave Kommel)

The nondescript home of Jenkins Competition in Malvern, Pennsylvania, was built to Bill's specifications back in 1973. The Grump told me that match race cash paid for this build. Imagine the stories if those walls could talk. (Author's Collection)

inch and capable of pushing the Monza to record-setting 8.50 times at 160 mph.

Jenkins's interests in drag racing began to wane as the decade drew to a close. After 1978, he campaigned Camaros exclusively in legal competition, all in the name of finicky NHRA weight breaks. After Lombardo left in 1979, Jenkins counted Ray Allen and Joe Lepone Jr. as drivers. The last *Grumpy's Toy* Camaro ran in 1983. Jenkins had been performing research and development for Chevrolet for some time, which continued well into the 1990s. Going back to the mid-1970s, Bill was instrumental in the development of the turbo head to the point that Chevrolet Engineer Ron Sperry referred to Bill as "the

father of the turbo head." Bill stated he had free reign at Saginaw, where he went during development of the Bowtie head. There he had the water bores modified to allow additional room to port. Jenkins's ties to Chevrolet paid dividends for the manufacturer, as Grumpy saved them millions in research and development, design, and manufacturing costs.

Emerging from the long shadow cast by the Grump were drivers such as Frank Iaconio, Warren Johnson, Reher, Morrison, and Shepherd. All were eager to pick up the Bowtie gauntlet and run with it. The body of choice became the second-generation Camaro, and in Pro Stock, there were plenty of them to cheer.

Royce Freeman

Royce Freeman was an early Pro Stock competitor who seemed to fly under the radar and grabbed wins while doing so. He joined Pro Stock in 1970 and teamed with Jim Hayter to campaign a 1968 Camaro. Based out of Lindsay, Oklahoma, Royce followed with a 1969 Camaro that broke more than he cared to remember. He was almost ready to throw in the towel in 1972, but then the NHRA announced that small-block-powered compacts could compete in Pro Stock.

Royce commissioned Don Hardy to build the Vega that Royce pulled from the lot of the family's Chevrolet dealership. Royce himself built the 331-ci engine that featured the best of parts from Edelbrock, Holley, General Kinetics, and American Heads. A BorgWarner 4-speed and a coilover 12-bolt housing 5.17 gears initially backed the Vega.

Royce, a member of the Texas Pro Stock Association, dominated in 1972 and won the first five races of 1973 before it gave him the boot. He updated the Vega in 1973; he set the engine back and added a Lenco and four-link suspension. Times in the 9.30s became common and helped Royce earn a

number of AHRA national events.

Royce left Pro Stock behind at the end of 1975 and built an A/SM 1967 Camaro. A B/SM 323-ci 1967 Chevy II followed before Royce retired from driving. The Vega was sold to a gentleman in San Antonio. Royce searched for the car years later and was told it had been crushed.

These days Royce is part of his son's Elite Motorsports and runs Pro Stock with Erica Enders in the driver's seat of the team's Camaro. Erica has won two NHRA World Championships for the team.

Royce Freeman campaigned his Don Hardy–built Vega through 1974. He loved beating on the Mopars and made a lot of money match racing them. Royce ran mainly AHRA races due to the fact there were an abundance of tracks in his area. (Author's Collection)

Wally Booth

Wally Booth, who was hot on Jenkins's heels with his own 1968 Camaro, played runner-up at the Springnationals in 1970 to the 'Cuda of Sox & Martin. Powering the Camaro to bottom 10s was an iron-block iron-head 427 put together by Dick Arons. Both Wally and Dick avoided the aluminum counter parts, as they felt the aluminum "walked around" too much and lost seal. With the NHRA Pro Stock rule that stated cars can be no older than three years, Booth found himself in the position of having to build a new car for the 1971 season.

Instead of starting from square one and working the bugs out of a new ride, Wally chose to update his current ride. In conjunction with Port Huron Custom Auto, Wally replaced the fenders, doors, quarter panels, dashboard, and other required items to convert his Camaro into a 1969.

Wally debuted the reskinned car at the 1971 NHRA Winternationals, where he made the final round but once again fell to Ronnie Sox. The Camaro qualified as the quickest Chevy at the race and became the first Chevy Pro Stocker to hit the 140 mph mark. Booth's best time for the aging car was a 9.72 at 141.95 mph. He ran the Camaro through the summer before he

In 1970, Booth's 1968 Camaro was one of the best-running Chevys in Pro Stock. Instead of building a new car for 1971 to adhere to NHRA's three-year rule, he rebodied his existing Camaro as a 1969. (Author's Collection)

debuted a second-generation Camaro at Indy. There, Booth survived until the third round of eliminations. At Milan Raceway that fall, Booth cranked out a 9.53 at 143.78 mph, which at the time, was the quickest time turned by a NHRA-legal Chevy Pro Stocker. Booth ran the Camaro through the end of 1971 before he jumped ship and joined AMC to race on its dime.

The beautiful Rat Pack 1976 Vega belonged to Michigan's Andy Mannarino. Wally Booth borrowed it to run at the 1976 NHRA Winternationals. Word reached Wally that the NHRA had plans to ban the fabricated heads he was running on his AMC Hornet. Wolverine built the chassis for the Vega. (Photo Courtesy Todd Wingerter)

Frank Iaconio

Frank Iaconio was another graduate of the 1960s Junior Stock and ran a fuel-injected 4-speed-equipped '57 business coupe. Frank won the Super Stock Nationals with the *Banana 1* in 1969, and took home $10,000 in cash and a new Cougar Eliminator, a car given by the event sponsor Air-Lift. Frank had no use for the Cougar and immediately sold it.

In 1971, the NHRA revised its rules and eliminated the use of the 4-speed transmission in the '57 Chevy. Frank then trialed a Powerglide in the car but felt he lost his competitive edge. He parted with the *Banana 1* and briefly took over driving the 1962 Plymouth of friends Tom Callahan and Frank Sulc.

In 1972, he returned to running a car of his own in the form of an SRD-built Pro Stock Vega. Initially powering the compact was a punched-out 327, which was built by Frank, a self-taught man who went into business after graduating high school. He worked out of his parents' garage before he opened the doors of his own shop in Totawa, New Jersey.

In 1974, he teamed with Ray Allen, a longtime friend who shared in driving chores. After he crashed the Vega, Frank regrouped and returned with Allen and Ritchie Schultz to campaign an SRD Monza. Each contributed $15,000 to the cause, which covered the cost of the car, a spare engine, and a transmission. They debuted the Monza six weeks before Indy 1976, and by Labor Day the car was tuned in. Frank powered through a tough field to meet the AMC Hornet of Wally Booth in the final.

Booth had been giving Pro Stock competition headaches all season with his Hornet thanks to a pair of sliced and diced heads that vastly improved horsepower output. In the final, Frank and his 323-ci Monza cut the light a little too close and lost with an 8.81. A small consolation to Frank was when the Monza was voted best appearing pro car. Frank and company ran the Monza through 1978 and retired the car with a total of five runner-up finishes and a win at the 1978 Gators.

Frank and Ray debuted a Don Ness–built Camaro in 1979, won two national events that season, and were runners-up at two more. They continued to rely upon their trusted 323-ci engine through 1980 and garnered two more runner-up finishes. In 1981, weight breaks directed Frank to run a de-stroked big-block that measured 360 ci. The new year also saw Frank going it alone after he bought Ray's share of the partnership. Ray exercised his options and spent 1981 driving for Grumpy

This 283-ci 283-hp '57 model 150 established Frank Iaconio as a force to be reckoned with. The Chevy defeated the nation's toughest to win the Super Stock Nationals in 1969. Frank's winning prize was a new Mercury Cougar Eliminator, which he promptly sold. (Photo Courtesy Carl Rubrecht)

Jenkins. Frank faired okay and won a pair of nationals events and played runner-up at one more.

Ray's gig with Jenkins never worked out, and he was back on a commission-type basis with Frank in 1982. Revised NHRA Pro Stock rules in 1982 said farewell to weight breaks and hello to 500 maximum cubic inches and a 2,350-pound minimum weight. The new rules went into effect at the season-opening Winternationals, a race Frank initially considered not attending.

"I was dynoing my engines at John Hoffman's and was hearing Reher-Morrison was making big numbers. The car and trailer were already out West, as I kept them at Roger Lamb's after the World Finals and just shipped the engines home. I dyno'd the motors, shipped them west, and tested at Orange prior to the Winters." In an understatement, Frank said the car, "Ran okay and we ended up winning the race." Frank defeated Lee Shepherd in the final with a 7.82. "We didn't know what to expect [with 500 ci]. We went from 8.60s to 7.80s." Frank followed with a win at Indy.

He immediately sold the Camaro to someone in Wisconsin and picked up his new Don Ness 1983 Camaro. He debuted the third-generation Camaro at the World Finals. This was Frank's most successful car and probably should have won the world title. Frank was ahead in points going in and qualified number one. In the first round he faced Reid Whisnant. Who knows whether it was a fault on the tree, but Reid was way down the track

Frank's Vega started out as a 1972 built by SRD and updated prior to the 1974 season with a new nose. Ray Allen drove the car occasionally before he finally teamed with Frank. (Photo Courtesy Michael Pottie)

Ray Allen helped pull wrenches on the Monza while Frank manned the controls. Ray is caught here doing his thing at Indy in 1976, where Frank drove the still-fresh Monza to a runner-up finish. (Photo Courtesy Dan Williams)

The Iaconio-Allen Monza played runner-up to Glidden here at the 1977 Fallnationals and again at the same meet in 1978. Midway through the 1978 season, the Monza was the quickest small-block Chevy Pro Stocker, recording 8.50 times. (Photo Courtesy Larry Pfister)

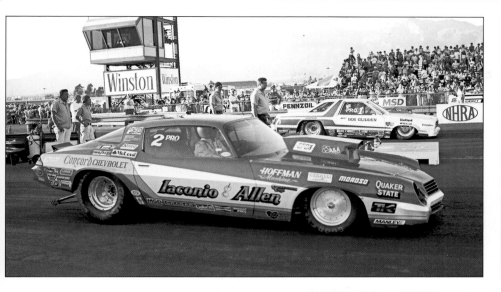

As a new decade dawned, Chevy Pro Stock took on a new look with Frank Iaconio's Reher-Morrison-Shepherd stepping to the forefront. Here at Ontario, Iaconio faces nemesis Bob Glidden. It's interesting to note in this 1981 photo that big name sponsors have yet to infiltrate Pro Stock. (Photo Courtesy Steve Reyes)

At the 1982 season opening Winternationals, Frank Iaconio defeated Lee Shepherd in the final with a 7.83 at 174 mph. That set a new class record and rang in the age of 7-second Pro Stocks. (Photo Courtesy Steve Reyes)

before Frank got a green. "He left early but never got a red light." The official refused to rerun the race and Frank lost the championship to Reher-Morrison.

Frank ran the Camaro through 1984 before he joined the Kenny Bernstein Budweiser team with a Ford Thunderbird. He ran the Thunderbird through 1986 before he set out on his own in 1987 with a new Thunderbird. The exercise proved to be too expensive and the car was sold. He came to his senses and ran a Super Shop–sponsored Firebird. In 1990, he bought a Don Ness Cutlass and ran it until he retired from driving in 1998.

Joe Satmary

Joe Satmary's career in Pro Stock ran a brief 10 years, but during those years he consistently finished in the NHRA top 10. He exclusively ran Chevys and did it all on

his own dime without a major sponsor. Joe started racing around 1963 when he was in the service and stationed at Bunker Hill Air Force Base. Shortly after he returned from service, he opened a Sunoco station in Highland, Indiana, where he partnered with Roger Burnett to campaign a Chevy-powered 1932 Studebaker Gasser. He next teamed with Mike Seltzer to run a Chevy II powered by an aluminum 427, aptly named *We-Haul*. In 1968, the pair ran with a 1967 Camaro and racked up the miles match racing and at AHRA events. Powered by a ZL1, and later a 454, the car featured a fiberglass front end and a Logghe front suspension.

Stepping up to Pro Stock in 1970, the aging Camaro was sold off and a new 1970½ Camaro was purchased from Blaskovich Chevrolet in East Chicago. To help recover costs, all the unwanted parts were stripped from

Originally campaigned by Butch Simpson, this Camaro was purchased by Mike Seltzer after Butch passed. Mike and Joe ran the car mainly in AHRA competition into 1970. Joe is seen here running AHRA SS/Eliminator. The car was later sold to a buyer in St. Louis. (Author's Collection)

With the advent of NHRA weight breaks, fewer cubic inches meant less weight, and Joe's big-blocks shrank in size as the decade went on. By incorporating a 348 crank, cubic inches dropped down to the 366 range while the use of a 409 crank generally gave Joe's rat motors 390 ci or more. Match race engines ran 454 inches and larger. Joe almost exclusively used cast-iron blocks as he, like others, found the aluminum blocks moved around too much and sealed poorly. Joe relied upon Van Senus in Hammond, Indiana, to perform pretty much all of his machine work. When it came to the heads, hundreds of hours were spent on the flow bench to search for that elusive power. Air Flow Research, one of Joe's few sponsors, has to get credit for hours spent helping out.

By the middle of the decade, Joe was running his operation out of a rented three-car garage. He had all the necessary equipment at hand (lathe, presses, etc.) to do all his own research and development and engine building. He debuted a new orange and white Camaro in 1973, which was a B&B chassis car that regularly qualified in the middle of the pack. The car made a few final-round appearances before it was sold to Richie Zul in 1978. Shortly after, Zul used the car to win the NHRA Springnationals.

the new car and sold back to the dealer. Seltzer and Satmary debuted the Camaro with a 0.030-over 427 backed by a Chrysler 4-speed and a mono-leaf-supported Dana 60 rear end with slapper bars.

Satmary drove the car to numerous AHRA events in 1971, and in 1972 ended the season second in points. Late in 1972, the guys had Ronnie Kaplin update the car with a tube chassis, aluminum floors, a four-link rear suspension, and Pinto rack up front.

The year 1973 was busy for Joe, as he briefly campaigned a Vega in conjunction with the Camaro. Built with the help of his brother Robert, the Vega debuted at the NHRA Winternationals but never made it out of the first round. Helping with the driving chores was Bill White, who worked alongside Joe at the station. Dave Atkin, formerly a driver with the Bill Hielscher team, moved north and spent some seat time in the Vega as well. The mouse motor in the Vega gave way to a 427 that propelled the car to 9-second times. The car proved to be a handful, so Joe parked it and focused his attention on the better-handling Camaro.

Joe's career in Pro Stock got off to a great start at an AHRA race when he defeated the Camaro of Jim Hayter in the final at Green Valley in May 1971. He finished the year with three more final-round appearances. (Photo Courtesy John Foster Jr.)

If a small-block won't do, then we'll stuff in a big-block. That's exactly what Joe Satmary did. The Vega's factory engine bay and frame rails left no room for headers, so Joe devised his own exhaust outlets. The car ran 9.60s in B/Gas at the IHRA Winter Nationals in 1973, a reported 0.5 below the class record. (Photo Courtesy Steve Reyes)

Satmary qualified number two here at Sanair in 1978 but fell in the first. Though it's tough to see on this car, the Tuff Rabbit name on the quarter panel came with the car and was the nickname of a Chicago area gent who helped out financially. (Photo Courtesy Bob Boudreau)

Always a favorite, underdog Joe Satmary took advantage of the weight breaks and ran incredible shrinking big-blocks in his 1973 Camaro. Seen here at Ontario Speedway in 1977, Joe had a new ride in 1978. (Photo Courtesy Dave Kommel)

Next up was the *Tuff Rabbit* 1973 Camaro purchased from Phil "Scrubs" Zobel. Along with the new car came a new partner in Harry Cannon. Joe made a good showing with the new car and qualified well into the pack at most shows and gained a few final-round appearances. The Camaro was updated in 1978 with new BFN fiberglass panels and a new blue-and-white paint scheme. Joe's best showing with the freshened car came at the U.S. Nationals in 1978, where he lost in the final to Bob Glidden. Joe occasionally defeated Glidden on their shared Division 3 tracks but couldn't pull it off on a national level.

The final go-round for Joe came in 1980 when he teamed with Jon Weaver. The two often butted heads in division races with Jon coming out on the losing end more times than not, and as the saying goes, if you can't beat 'em, join 'em. Jon offered up his Don Ness Camaro while Joe provided the 366-ci motor. The last showing for Joe on the national level was at the NHRA World Finals in October 1980, where he fell to eventual runner-up, Frank Iaconio. The partnership between Joe and Jon, which was rocky pretty much from the get-go, dissolved immediately after the finals. By that point, Joe's personal life was also on a quick downward spiral. Financial woes caused him to sell off pretty much everything he owned after he found himself on the wrong side of the law. He died a broken man in 1996 at the age of 54.

Richie Zul

Richie Zul of Lindenhurst, New York, was the consummate underdog who always managed to do more with less. Though known far and wide for his dedication to Chevy, Richie actually started his racing career behind the wheel of a Hemi-powered 1953 Studebaker. He ran the car at Long Island's Islip through the early 1960s before he cashed it in for a small-block Chevy-powered 1958 Studebaker wagon. The small-block soon gave way to a 425-hp 409 and 4-speed combo. With the addition of a straight axle, Richie was ready to take on the Gassers. He cleaned house with the wagon, but after he was inched out by an L79 Nova, he knew what his next ride had to be. He ran the Nova in Super Stock through 1969 but changed direction in 1970 with the introduction of NHRA Pro Stock.

Richie built a 1969 Camaro that debuted at the Summernationals in 1972 and promptly got his "ass whooped," he said. The first runs netted 10.0 times, which were just a little off the 9.60 pace. Still, it was a first step and not a bad one for an independent who, in his own words, had no money and relied upon scrapyard parts.

The Camaro was powered by a stock-inch L88 427 that housed factory rods, pistons, aluminum heads, a General Kinetics cam, twin 660 Holleys, Edelbrock intake, Stahl Headers, Mallory magneto, and little else. Backing the mill was a T-10 transmission and Dana 60 rear end supported by leaf springs and bolt-on traction bars.

The car was just coming alive when it was stolen shortly before the 1973 Summernationals. The theft nearly wiped Richie out. Along with the car went the truck, spare engine, tools, and everything. He had just installed a Lenco transmission five days before and recorded low-9 times. By Richie's calculations, the theft set him back about two years.

Grumpy Jenkins, who had been watching Zul's rise, took Richie under his wing and the relationship proved beneficial to Zul. "Jenkins was kind of my mentor. We both came from a similar background where you scraped by and did it all yourself." There's no denying both were

Richie did okay with his first Pro Stocker, this 427-powered 1969 Camaro, considering, as he put it, "doing what you thought you knew, but you didn't know nothing." Pegged as the fastest big-block Camaro in the nation at one time, Zul rang 9.20 ETs out of the car. (Photo Courtesy Michael Pottie)

self-taught men with great minds for engineering. Jenkins loaned Zul his 1970½ Camaro, which Richie eventually bought for "about" $5,000. Along with the car, Jenkins gave him a T-10 transmission, a manifold, two carbs, and some rims and tires. Richie saw his share of success with the car through 1976. Running a 409 incher (4.31 bore x 3.50 stroke), the Camaro was the first big-block car to run in the 8s, having done so at Englishtown, where it recorded an 8.98 time. Richie closed

> **"Jenkins was kind of my mentor. We both came from a similar background where you scraped by and did it all yourself."**
> – Richie Zul

the 1974 season number 5 in the Pro Stock standings and won the Division 1 points championship. The same year the Camaro received its first major upgrades when SRD Race Cars set the engine back the legal amount. He swapped the leaf springs and slapper bars for a four-link and wheel tubs.

Richie's success continued in 1975 with an IHRA Pro Stock win and a runner-up finish at the Nationals. He finished both the 1975 and 1976 seasons number 7 in NHRA Pro Stock. He continued to do it on his own and supported his habit and family by match racing, running Frank LeSueur's Division 1 Pro Stock circuit, and building a few engines for others. Richie suffered through a lack of a major sponsor, but he did get some help with parts. Richie saved where he could and recalled the days when he'd follow the hemi guys around and pick up their discarded warm-up spark plugs. A toothbrush and a little lacquer thinner had them as good as new. Jenkins was another person who Richie could rely upon. "Jenkins liked to throw stuff at me and see me make it work."

Prior to the NHRA World Finals in 1976, Richie received a call from Reher and Morrison. They wanted him to drive their rebuilt Monza. Lee Shepherd had crashed the Don Ness–built car at Indy and, according to Richie, couldn't get a grip on the rebuilt car. "The car didn't handle well. You'd make a pass and the car would go left and right." Modifications were made and Richie signed on to drive the car through the 1977 season. His well-used Camaro, minus the engine, was sold to Dennis Ferrara. Though national event wins escaped the newly formed team, they made a good showing and closed the 1977 season with a seventh-place finish. At the end of the season, Ritchie headed back to New York to run a new car of his own.

Richie bought the 1973 Camaro that Joe Satmary had been campaigning and ran it with the same "junk" he ran in his previous Camaro. Richie compared the car to the old Jenkins ride as night and day. "It was a great car with the right weight in the right spot and ran fast on any track."

With a few chassis mods, a little weight reduction, and a change in tire to a pair of 14x32s procured from Jenkins, the car laid down an 8.49 at 158 mph to qualify number one at Gainesville. Richie won the follow-up Springnationals and defeated the Pinto of Bob Glidden in the final with an 8.76 at 155.44 mph.

With the NHRA five-year rule taking effect, the Satmary car needed to be replaced in 1979. Weighing his options, Richie stuck with the favorable Camaro body and called on SRD Race Cars to build the car. Power for

Richie ran a cast-iron junkyard block with aluminum heads that measured 409 ci in his Camaro. At 7.00 pounds per cubic inch, the car weighed in at 2,860 pounds and managed 8-second times. Mini tubs and ladder bars controlled the hop. (Photo Courtesy Michael Pottie)

By the time this photo was shot in 1975 at a National Trail points meet, Zul's Camaro had been reworked by SRD. The engine was set back and rear wheel tubs were added. (Photo Courtesy Todd Wingerter)

Richie's final go in Pro Stock was with this SRD Camaro. Running a 354-ci big-block, Richie was the first to make the combo work and felt penalized by the NHRA for doing so. The frustration of NHRA weight breaks was enough for Richie to call it quits in 1979. (Photo Courtesy Michael Pottie)

the new Camaro came by way of a shrunken big-block that measured 354 ci. Richie was the first one to make the small-inch combo work and qualified 13th at Englishtown the first time out.

Richie was working out the combination when he joined up with Reher and Morrison. "I flew all my stuff out there because I thought I was going to have a career there." Richie figures Reher and Morrison "tweaked" his ideas and won their first world championship in 1980 with their own small-inch engine.

Richie's new Camaro was allowed to run at the 2,250-pound minimum, according to the NHRA's long wheelbase, small cubic inch rule. But it seemed like everyone complained after he qualified the car at Englishtown. By the time he got to Indy, he was told he had to run the 2,450-pound weight. "I didn't even unload the car. It barely qualified as it was. I had enough; I was beat and broke."

Lee "the General" Edwards

When conversation turns to Mountain Motor Pro Stock, Lee Edwards generally tops everyone's list. Lee

first started toying with big-blocks back in the late 1960s while running an A/Gas Anglia out of his automotive shop in Virginia. Lee's always been a Chevy guy and

Edwards found drag racing A/Gas during the latter half of the 1960s with this injected 427-powered Anglia. The next stop for the General was Pro Stock. (Photo Courtesy Bill Truby)

This is the way Pro Stocks were hauled in the beginning. Lee's first Pro Stock national event win came at the IHRA Winter Nationals in Lakeland, Florida, where he defeated Arlen Vanke in the final. The Camaro regularly ran 9.70s in 1972 at speeds approaching 140 mph. (Photo Courtesy Bill Truby)

Seeing that weight breaks favored the mouse motor Vega combo in 1972, Lee parked his Camaro and debuted this Don Hardy car in 1973. He returned to running big-blocks in 1975. (Photo Courtesy Steve Reyes)

The mouse propelled the Vega to a good showing in IHRA, where the Culver, Virginia–based Lee focused most of his attention. Gebler headers and a General Kinetics cam placed the Vega well into the 9s. Pro Stock rules of the day dictated a stock front frame. (Photo Courtesy Steve Reyes)

started back in the early 1950s with a Chevy-powered 1939 Plymouth.

He built his first Pro Stocker, a big-block-powered Camaro, in 1971 and competed in IHRA competition. The Camaro gave Lee his first taste of national event victory in 1972, when he defeated the Plymouth of Arlen Vanke at the IHRA Winter Nationals. Lee side-stepped into the world of small-blocks in 1973 when he debuted a Don Hardy Vega. In the world of weight breaks, the small-block Vega seemed the favorable way to go. Not so much for Lee though. The man had learned big-blocks like no other and returned in 1975 with a big-block-powered Don Hardy Camaro.

While the Camaro ran NHRA, Lee had Kenny Hodger build him an IHRA Vega. When the IHRA went to a 2,350-pound, "whatever cubic inch you want" format in 1976, Lee was ready. The Vega was Lee's first Mountain Motor car that ran a 490 cubic incher. The engine went together with a passenger car block with a long stroke and a few extra head gaskets to prevent the valves from caving in the pistons.

Lee was the first star of IHRA's Mountain Motor Pro Stock and won the championship in 1977 and 1978. He had the 1979 title all but wrapped up heading into the final race of the season and only needed to win one round to take his third championship. Warren Johnson was hot on his heels, but it took Lee going out in the first round and Johnson winning the meet for Lee to grab the title. Wouldn't

you know it—Lee blew a tire in the first round, which cost him the needed win, and Johnson sailed on to win the meet.

By the late 1970s, cubic inches had climbed to 570 and were well on their way past 600 when a Rodeck block and a later P&S block were used. P&S created an aluminum tall-deck block that placed the camshaft 1/4 inch higher in the block to allow additional room for stroking. In an interview with Competition Plus, Lee stated that early on, "There was nothing out there to buy. We had to make it all. We used stock blocks and made the best out of what we had to work with. Things got pretty inno-

Battle of the big-blocks at the 1976 NHRA Winternationals saw Lee fall to Warren Johnson in round one. These were just two racers who ran the big-block/Camaro combos in an attempt to take advantage of the NHRA's wonky weight breaks. (Photo Courtesy Dave Kommel)

Lee Edwards's 1976 Vega, built by Hodger Engineering, was pretty innovative for the day. The body could be stripped from the chassis in minutes for ease of maintenance. The car is captured here for posterity at the IHRA Summernationals. It was the beginning of a new era in Pro Stock: minimum weight and all the cubic inches you could build. (Photo Courtesy Dan Williams)

vative. But I didn't mess around. I just made them as big as I could make them. That was one of the keys to my success."

Lee continued to be a dominating force in IHRA competition through 1979. He retired from active racing in 1980 after campaigning a Hodger-built 1978 Camaro. Today he is recognized as the IHRA's number-one Mountain Motor racer. As of this writing, Lee Edwards Racing Engines in Calverton, Virginia, is building mega-inch motors for some of the nation's quickest and fastest drag cars and tractor pullers.

Warren Johnson

Warren Johnson was a virtual unknown outside of Division 5 when in 1976, he finished the season number two in NHRA Pro Stock. I doubt anyone would have thought this guy would one day be the winningest driver in Pro

Johnson's gorgeous A/MP 1940 Chevy was powered by a big-block. The Stovebolt was well known and feared in his home state of Minnesota. Note the "Peerless Racing Engines" on the hood. Within a couple years, Johnson was in business for himself. (Author's Collection)

Johnson debuted his first Camaro Pro Stocker in 1971. A 427 4-speed and a 12-bolt with slapper bars was a good start. By the end of the 1972 season, the Camaro had recorded a best of 9.38. Camaro enthusiasts will note the RS bumpers on the non-RS front end. (Photo Courtesy John Foster Jr.)

George Wepplo built Warren's Vega in 1973. Power for the car came by way of a de-stroked big-block. The pretty paint was laid on by Pat Bonnet. Warren dedicated his full attention to Pro Stock in 1975. (Photo Courtesy Tommy Shaw)

For Warren Johnson, Ontario 1976 was a long way from 1964, which was when he first got serious about drag racing with a Modified Production '57 Chevy. At Ontario, Warren fell early to eventual World Champ Larry Lombardo. Johnson and his Don Ness Camaro closed the season as number two in Pro Stock. (Photo Courtesy Dave Kommel)

The 500-plus-ci Monte Carlo was built by Warren Johnson and owned by Jerome Bradford. In 1981, the Monte went into the record books as the AHRA's first 7-second Pro Stocker when Johnson recorded a 7.93 at 176.81 mph. (Photo Courtesy Jim Kampmann)

Stock. His climb to the upper echelons of Pro Stock began with a big-block-powered 1971 Camaro that debuted at Indy that year. He supported his drag racing and growing family as a steel worker and by operating his Competition Engine Service on the side. As time permitted, he attended evening courses to obtain an engineering degree. In 1976, he turned pro and focused full time on his drag racing.

Johnson debuted his Minnesota Custom Fabrication George Wepplo tube-chassis Vega in 1973. Powered by a de-stroked big-block that measured 398 ci, the Vega, for a time, was considered the fastest big-block Chevy in Pro Stock with an 8.91 at 154 mph. Johnson's early success came in AHRA competition, where at Tulsa in August 1974 the Vega defeated the Dodge of Larry Huff. Johnson parked the quirky handling Vega after he debuted a Don Ness Camaro in 1975. It was a long time coming but Warren won his first points meet in August 1975. Held at

Bison Dragway in Winnipeg, Canada, he defeated John Hagen in the final and recorded times of 9.21 at 148.51 mph. In 1976, Johnson won all five Division 2 points meets, and at the end of the season held the class mile per hour record with a 158.73 mph.

Determining just who would be the Pro Stock World Champion in 1976 boiled down to the season-ending World Finals. It would either be Larry Lombardo in the *Grumpy's Toy* Monza or Johnson and his Camaro. Lombardo qualified with an off-pace 8.93, which forced him to face Johnson in the first round. If Johnson could have defeated Lombardo and won two more rounds, the title would have been his. What could have been if it weren't for a sticking line loc in Johnson's Camaro. Still, it was a close one with Lombardo winning with a 9.00 to Johnson's quicker 8.91. Lombardo took the World Championship and Johnson had to wait until 1982 before he had his first NHRA national event win.

An NHRA national event win was a long time coming for Johnson, who won three of them in 1982. His Chevy-powered Olds Starfire was designed by Warren himself and constructed at Arrow Dynamics in Colorado. To say Johnson was ready for the world of 500-ci Pro Stock would be an understatement. (Photo Courtesy Dave Kommel)

In the meantime, Johnson racked up the wins in IHRA competition and won world titles in 1979 and 1980. In 1981, he teamed with Jerome Bradford to campaign a 500-inch Monte Carlo to do battle against the 600-inch Shotgun Fords in IHRA. Capable of 7.80s, the experience he gained helped Johnson jump to instant stardom in 1982 when the NHRA adopted the IHRA-style Pro Stock format. Johnson and his Chevy-powered Olds Starfire won the Summernationals in 1982 over Lee Shepherd. It was a close one with Johnson just nipping Shepherd's 7.91 at 173.74 mph with a 7.90 at 174.41.

When Oldsmobile launched its drag racing program in 1983, Warren was the person chosen to spearhead the program. Warren can take credit for reworking the big-block Chevy to create the Drag Racing Competition Engine (DRCE), the go-to engine in GM Pro Stock.

The "Professor's" accolades are plenty. From a safety perspective, he brought innovations to Pro Stock in the form of restraints, roll cage, and suspension design. At the track, Johnson's "all-business" approach helped him earn six NHRA World titles. He became the first to run a Pro Stocker over 200, which happened at Virginia in 1997 when he hit 200.13 mph in his GM Performance Parts–sponsored Pontiac Firebird.

Reher, Morrison, and Shepherd

David Reher, Buddy Morrison, and Lee Shepherd (RMS) made their trek into the world of Pro Stock at NHRA's first Cajun Nationals in 1976. The trio had cashed in their potent modified Corvette and commissioned Don Ness to fabricate a chassis for their new Monza. Using their own 331-inch mill, Shepherd fought his way to the finals where he faced low-qualifier Wally Booth and his AMC Hornet. Booth had hit a best of 8.80

Richie weighed his options, sold the Camaro to Dennis Ferrara, and moved to Texas to drive for Reher-Morrison. His first outing in the rebuilt Monza was at the 1976 World Finals in Pomona. (Photo Courtesy Paul Johnson)

during qualifying, which was 0.11 quicker than the RMS Monza, but in the final, Shepherd caught Booth napping and laid a lead on him that he just couldn't make up. When the win light came on, Shepherd had won with a 9.07 at 151.77 mph to a quicker 8.88 at 153.32 mph.

Lee Shepherd crashed the Monza at the following Summernationals after a Heim joint broke, which sent the car into multiple rollovers. It's a credit to Ness that Lee walked away from the 8.86 at 152 mph run. The car was rebuilt and Richie Zul was stuck in the driver's seat to run the car through 1977. A shaken Shepherd spent a year running a Modified Camaro before he took back the Monza in 1978.

RMS debuted a Ness Camaro in 1979 and used the small-block-powered car to win a pair of AHRA national events. Feeling they had wrung all they could out of the engine, the team went to a 362-ci big-block (3.25 stroke) in 1980. They opened the new season by winning the AHRA Winternationals. They were well on their way to win the NHRA Championship, having won six national events, but lost the crown at the last race of the season due to a broken transmission. They rebounded in 1981 and won their first of four NHRA world titles.

RMS carried the number 2 in 1981 after a failed Lenco at the World Finals in 1980 cost them their first world title. The late Lee Shepherd is considered one of the best all-around Pro Stock competitors of our time in anyone's book. (Photo Courtesy Jim Kampmann)

Seven seconds to glory was the battle cry in 1982, as the NHRA tossed the confusing weight breaks and went with 2,350-pound minimum weight, 500-ci maximum rule. Thank the IHRA for forcing the NHRA's hand. In 1976, it was the first to eliminate weight breaks and go the big inch route. The winningest car in Pro Stock history bar none was the 1982 Reher and Morrison Camaro. While they relied upon a 500-ci for NHRA competition, the IHRA's mills ran from 615 to 638 ci. RMS nearly matched the NHRA results by winning three IHRA world titles in 1983, 1984, and 1985.

According to RMS historian Rick Voegelin, the secret to RMS success in 1982 and 1983 was the cylinder heads. The heads started life as Chevy C-port castings without water jackets. Shepherd went hog wild, angle milling and raising the ports and contouring. Coolant passages were drilled after the fact. Horsepower of the NHRA mill was just over 1,000.

Tragedy struck the RMS camp on March 11, 1985, when Lee Shepherd lost his life while testing at Ardmore Raceway. In NHRA competition, Lee had 29 national event wins and had been in the final round in 44 of the last 56 NHRA national events before his death.

Reher and Morrison did their best to carry on and brought in Bruce Allen as partner and driver. They won another 10 national events before they retired from active racing in 2005.

NHRA's first 500-ci world championship car belonged to Reher-Morrison-Shepherd. The team won six national events and played runner-up at five more to win their first of four consecutive championships in 1982. Don Ness built the chassis and earned his second of three Car Craft magazine's Pro Stock chassis builder awards. (Photo Courtesy Steve Reyes)

The winningest car in drag racing history was the Reher-Morrison third-generation Camaro. Running IHRA and NHRA competition, the car won 5 world championships and 24 national events between 1983 and 1985. (Photo Courtesy Steve Reyes)

★★☆ THE BEST OF THE REST ★★☆

There were just too many well-running Chevy Pro Stocks to list them all here, so this is a selection of the best of the rest. Chevy overcame the early Hemi dominance and held its ground when the Cleveland Fords of Bob Glidden, Dyno Don, and Gapp & Roush took over the category. These die-hard Chevy racers helped keep our hopes alive.

Driving the Fred Gibb's number-one ZL1 Camaro, Oklahoma-based Jim Hayter won the 1971 AHRA Pro Stock World Championship. The Camaro was initially driven by Herb Fox and Ray Sullins under the Fred Gibb/ Dick Harrell banner. Best ETs were in the 9.60s. (Photo Courtesy Steve Reyes)

Butch Leal built this Camaro at Bill Thomas Race Cars in the spring of 1970 after he failed to reach a desired deal with Chrysler. Butch ran the Chevy into 1971 and won major races at Carlsbad, Riverside, and Phoenix before Chrysler finally loosened the purse strings and supplied him with a Duster. As Butch noted, "The Camaro was built to help me land the Chrysler deal." (Photo Courtesy James Handy)

Steve Kanuika is probably better known for his Pennsylvania-area speed shops than his track cars. His engine building was second to none and brought success to many, including "Jungle Jim," who ran Kanuika engines in his Nova Funny Cars. Steve's most memorable drag car was this heads-up Camaro he built in 1969. Powered by a 427, the Camaro recorded high-9s in 1969. (Photo Courtesy Carl Rubrecht)

At the 1972 U.S. Nationals, Ray Allen in his Truppi-Kling SRD Vega, defeated the MIMI Vega driven by Rich Mirarcki in the Pro Stock final. The race lacked many big-name racers who instead chose to run the opposing PRA race. Allen's 327 Vega was the only Pro Stocker running in the 9.50s and won the event with a 9.58 at 141.50 mph. (Photo Courtesy Michael Pottie)

After successfully campaigning a '56 Chevy in Stock, Sonny Bryant moved to Pro Stock in 1971 with this home-built Camaro. His mill of choice was a 427 that he used to set the ET record in 1977 at 8.58. He and a few friends performed all the work on the car themselves, excluding the new front frame and suspension that was added in 1976 by M&S Race Cars. Sonny ran the car through 1981 before he debuted a Don Hardy 500-ci Firebird. He retired from active racing in 1984 and sold the car, trailer, et al. to start his crankshaft business. (Photo Courtesy Edelbrock LLC Archives)

Bill Blanding was a college professor out of New York who loved drag racing. In total, there were eight MIMI cars, all driven by Rich Mirarcki, starting with a Super Stock Camaro back in 1967. The final MIMI was this Fred Forkner–built Vega. Power came by way of a Booth-Arons–built 331-ci. A T-10 transmission and Dana rear completed the drivetrain. The Vega also saw duty running D/Altered. (Photo Courtesy Michael Pottie)

☆☆☆ THE BEST OF THE REST ☆☆☆

Division 1's Norm Fryer was responsible for building a number of potent Chevys. He liked his 427s. Prior to the heads-up Camaro, he ran a 427-powered 1966 Biscayne in Junior Stock. (Author's Collection)

Dave Strickler retired from drag racing at the end of 1973 after campaigning this 331-ci SRD Vega. Dave joined the Ammon R. Smith dealership team in the mid-1960s and worked himself up to the vice presidency before the dealership closed in the early 1980s. (Photo Courtesy Todd Wingerter)

Dutch Irrgang raced the "Jungle Jim" Vega wagon into 1974. Top Fuel racer Fred Forkner helped extensively with the build that included many leftover parts from the Funny Cars of "Jungle Jim." Powering the wagon was a 331-ci built by K&G Speed Associates. Dutch spent two years as Grumpy Jenkins's transmission guy and prepared his own BorgWarner Super T-10 4-speed. (Photo Courtesy Marlin Huss)

Running on a next-to-nil budget, Kevin Rotty, Frank Townsend, and Butch McDaniel did alright for themselves. Between 1973 and 1980, the Tucson-based team finished in the NHRA Pro Stock top 10 five times. In 1980, Rotty's last season behind the wheel, he finished number four in NHRA standings. Seen here in 1977, the Camaro is said to be running a 407-ci engine. (Photo Courtesy Larry Pfister)

Jegs entered the world of Pro Stock for the first time in 1973 with this Mark Campbell–driven Vega. The car, chassis, and mouse motor were all built in house at Jegs in Ohio. (Photo Courtesy Bob Martin)

Sam Gianino gave Pro Stock a shot in 1973 after he competed for a number of years in Street and Modified Eliminator. Through his career, Sam captured in the neighborhood of 30 class records. Customers of Gianino Race Engines in Detroit probably matched that number. National event wins for Sam included taking Street at the 1968 Nationals in his Executioner Corvette. He closed his career in a third-generation Pro Stock Firebird. This small-inch Vega featured a Wolverine chassis. (Photo Courtesy Bob Martin)

☆ ☆ ☆ THE BEST OF THE REST ☆ ☆ ☆

Rick DeLisi was a better car owner than driver. This one of two Waco Kid Monzas, seen here at the Grandnationals in 1978, was an SRD car that was later driven with much success by Dempsey Hardy in B/FX. Dempsey ran the car between 1979 and 1982 while Dennis Ferrara competed with the second Waco Monza in B/Econo Altered in 1979. In 1979, Rick drove a Don Ness Pro Stock Camaro. His drag race days came to a crashing end in 1980 when he and his brother were busted for drug smuggling. (Photo Courtesy Bob Boudreau)

Brad Yuill gives the Don Hardy chassis in his Monza a working here at the Fallnationals in 1977. Built in 1976 with a small-block, Yuill switched to a 381-ci big-block late in the year to take advantage of weight breaks. Brad and Mark, in a matching Camaro, combined for a total of 16 division points race wins and 5 division titles (Brad in 1976; Mark 1977, 1978, 1979, and 1981). The brothers retired from Pro Stock in 1988. (Photo Courtesy Larry Pfister)

Huston Platt stands his Chevy II up on its 11-inch Goodyears in this match against the 427 Mustang of Gene Lunsford. Platt ran an injected 396 stretched to 454 inches. Platt, who had been running Chevys since the 1950s, held true to the brand throughout his career. *(Photo Courtesy Alan Garletts)*

Chapter Six

The Funny Pages

The predecessors of today's Funny Cars were the mid-1960s Altered Wheelbase Stockers. Fighting against the limited tire technology of the day, builders solved their traction ills by shifting the front and rear suspension forward, which placed more of the car's weight on the rear. Who was the first to make these alterations? Who knows for sure, but Chevy racers were right there and jumped into the game with both feet. Through the decade, they'd more than hold their own against the Hemi Mopars and Cammer Fords. Things changed as tire technology improved and nitro loads increased. By the early 1970s, if you wanted reliability and consistency, aftermarket Hemis by Ed Donovan or Keith Black were the way to go. A few diehard Chevy racers tried to battle on but faced ever-increasing odds.

Kelly "the Professor" Chadwick

One of those meeting the Hemi onslaught was Kelly Chadwick. Kelly, nicknamed the Professor due to his teaching background, had an uncanny ability to school his drag race competition. Born in Jackson County, Oklahoma, in 1931, Kelly's initial interest in fast cars centered on NASCAR, but with the Southern tracks too far away, his interest soon turned to straight-line action. Kelly married in 1953 and the young couple briefly relocated to California, where he left his teaching behind and went to work for TRW. That summer he visited the quarter mile at Santa Ana and made his first pass in a 1952 Chevy. Kelly moved to Texas, returned to teaching, and visited local tracks through the late 1950s to hone his skills behind the wheel of a Power Pack '55 and later an A/Stock 270-hp '57.

In 1961, Kelly teamed with one of his old students, Don Hardy, and built a B/Gas 1932 Ford. Powered by an injected 301-inch Chevy, Kelly took class honors with

Kelly "the Professor" Chadwick of Floydada, Texas, won more matches than he ever lost. His 1964 Chevelle went through a number of changes and initially ran with a Z11 for power. (Photo Courtesy James Gipson)

the car at the AHRA Nationals in Green Valley in 1962. He won 24 straight eliminations at Amarillo and spent most of the season in the thick of the NHRA Division 4 points chase. It was during this period that Kelly became good friends with fellow Chevy diehard Dick Harrell. At times, the pair traveled from track to track together.

The Chadwick-Hardy partnership took a break in 1963 when Uncle Sam sent Don off on a tour of Alaska. Kelly took a brief hiatus from racing and pulled the engine from the '32 and sold the car to focus on a growing family and

*Kelly Chadwick and Don Hardy led the NHRA points race for a good part of the 1961 season before a broken connecting rod set them back. Though they fell out of contention, the car did go on to win B/Gas at the AHRA Nationals at Green Valley in September 1962. The Ford was sold to Johnny Hodges shortly after, where it was renamed **Sassy Sue** before disappearing. (Photo Courtesy John Bergener/ Bill Fronterhouse)*

his teaching career. The hiatus didn't last long, as Harrell suggested he build a new car and cash in on the growing match race craze sweeping the nation. Dick told him that he had a couple of spare Z11 engines and all he needed was to find a car. He found one at Oden Chevrolet in Floydada, Texas. Oden provided a showroom-fresh Chevelle, and with longtime friend and engine builder James Gipson in tow, the pair went to work to put together a winning combination. They ran A/FX and plenty of match races with the car to rack up a 70 percent win percentage through the remainder of the year.

The car spent a lot of time at Gipson's shop in Amarillo over the winter of 1964–1965. Kelly had Lyden Moss alter the wheelbase and move the front suspension up 3 inches and the rear up 6 inches. Kelly then called on Dick Sheffield to spray on the new red paint. During the same period, the Z11 gave way to an all-new-for-1965 Mark IV 396 engine. Though advertised on the car as a 427, after a bore and stroke it actually measured out to 440 inches. The engine was so new that Kelly couldn't get his hands on a long-block from Chevrolet and had to buy a complete car to get the motor. He purchased a 375-hp Impala, pulled the motor, installed a 409, and sold the car back to the dealer. The price we must pay to play.

Prior to installing the 396, parts were sent to California, where the crank was stroked by Delta Machine, pistons were made, and Joe Mondello worked over the heads. An experimental Sig Erson cam actuated the valves. A Muncie transmission and Pontiac rear end completed the drivetrain. With times hitting the 10.50s at over 130, Kelly's win percent jumped to 90 in 1965.

A Chevy II followed in 1966, and when Don Hardy returned from service, the pair went to work on building the new match racer in Kelly's home garage. Some say that this is when Don really got involved in chassis building and credit Chadwick's Chevy II as the first "Don Hardy" build. Hardy took over building the engines for Chadwick until business took off for him in 1968.

> **"The first time [Kelly Chadwick] blipped the throttle to clean it out, he picked up the left front wheel. The car would just explode when you hit the throttle."**
> – Bryan Teal

Kelly's son Royce vividly recalled the Chevy II. "They fired it up one night in the garage around 11 o'clock. My bed was vibrating across the floor every time they revved it up. A neighbor wasn't too impressed. He came knocking on the door the next morning, threatening my dad that he better not do that again."

Royce obviously loved his dad but Dick Harrell was his favorite racer. "My dad's and Dick's car were identical. My dad was so mad at me because I had a little car, a Chevy II, I used to play with in my room and I painted Dick Harrell's name on it. I've got a letter from when I was a kid, and in it Dad says, 'I put your boy Dick Harrell on the trailer.'"

Kelly generally ran a 70-percent load of nitro through

the 440 until Delmar Heinelt, who drove *Seaton's Shaker*, showed him how to run it on a 98-percent load. Bryan Teal, who crewed with Chadwick, said, "The first time he blipped the throttle to clean it out, he picked up the left front wheel. The car would just explode when you hit the throttle. He bent some rods one time at Odessa just cleaning it out in the staging lanes. It ran a little over 150 at 9.30s loaded."

Kelly had Hardy build him a Camaro in 1967, but fans refused to give up on the Chevy II. Kelly ran both cars simultaneously, and given a choice, promoters chose the Chevy II. Kelly finally had to tell them he wasn't racing the Chevy II anymore. The Camaro was powered by another injected, bored, and stroked 427 and immediately ran 10 mph faster and about a half-second quicker than the Chevy II. A blower was added in 1968 and ran 22 mph faster on Kelly's first pass. With plans to build a second Camaro, fellow Funny Car pilot Ray Sullins was hired. When plans fell through on the second car, Sullins stayed to pull wrenches.

Drag racing full-time now, Kelly took up a sales position at Steakley Chevrolet in Dallas to fill his downtime. A sponsorship agreement was worked out with the dealer and part of the deal was that Kelly would run a door car. A 375-hp 396 Camaro was pulled from inventory and prepared by Don Hardy. The 396 ran all GM parts and initially had a twin 4-barrel setup on a Weiand intake for AHRA competition. That setup failed to meet expectations and was replaced with a factory high-rise and 800 Holley.

The car was initially driven by Coke Royal, but the job was passed to Ray Sullins when work prevented Coke from traveling. Ray said, "Kelly had booked the car up and down the East Coast and all over the Midwest. I took a truck out of Steakley inventory to haul the Camaro, and between March 15th and September 1st I logged 75,000 miles on the odometer. The Camaro was raced in 1969 only and ran 10.90s. I built Kelly a Super Stock 1969 Camaro before I went to the Harrell-Gibb race team in 1969."

The new Camaro was powered by a 0.060-over 396 with a similar amount shaved off the top of the block and pistons. When installed in

In 1965, the Chevelle received a fiberglass front clip, roll cage, leaf-spring rear suspension, and altered wheelbase. With wheels up and with each gear pull, the Chevelle hit 10.90 times. (Photo Courtesy James Gipson)

Kelly Chadwick and Pete Seaton battle it out at Bakersfield in 1966. This was the first year where Altered Wheelbase cars ran at the U.S. Fuel & Gas Championship meet. Kelly and the deuce were in such demand in 1966 that he quit his teaching position to focus on drag racing. (Photo Courtesy Forrest Bond)

Kelly's Camaro featured a steel body mounted on a Don Hardy chassis. Fiberglass fenders, doors, and decklid replaced the steel counterparts. The rear suspension was moved forward 8 inches, and the lengthened front end saw the front moved some 15 inches forward. As a result, the car rolled on a 115-inch wheelbase. (Photo Courtesy Richard Nicholson)

Kelly's Camaro rode on a 124-inch wheelbase chassis. Harnessing the power of the 427 were 13x16 M&H Racemasters. The Ron Pellegrini body features candy red paint by Corky Larson. (Photo Courtesy Carl Rubrecht)

the car, the engine was raised and set back in the chassis. Initial fire was through factory exhaust manifolds, as they couldn't get headers to fit the "bogus" setup. Their first trip with the Camaro was to California for the AHRA Winternationals, where they had Jardine build a set of headers for the motor.

Another interesting feature of the car was that its rear end was relocated 2 inches forward. With the Camaro's short rear overhang, this no doubt helped in the traction department. The Camaro recorded 10.70 times at 134 mph on its initial outing.

Don Hardy built Kelly his first flip-up Funny Car, a Camaro, in 1969. Probably Kelly's most successful car, the Camaro won the Coca-Cola Cavalcade of Stars F/C series in 1969 and had Don Hardy back to pull wrenches. The Cavalcade was a 35-race, 8-car program that featured some of the nation's top cars and drivers.

In 1970, Don Hardy retired to build the chassis and Ray Sullins returned to the Chadwick camp to fill the void as crew chief. With Ray's help, Kelly repeated his Cavalcade series win. As Ray recalled, the pair ran well over 100 dates in 1970. For power, the Funny Car used the taller Chevy truck block. With a stroke, the engine measured out to 494 inches.

"It would be necessary to grind out the bottom of each cylinder for rod clearance. You'd grind into the water jacket and have to braze it back up. Running the tall deck, spacers were made to make the intake manifold fit, as well as the magneto. Kelly never lost a truck block and knew how to make them last. He was easy on parts and had a feel for the car that few have. He knew when something was set to happen and shut off before damage was done."

A new JE Fiberglass Camaro was built by Hardy for Kelly in 1971, and it won more than its share of match races and

Ray Sullins and Don Hardy were responsible for putting together this L78 Camaro for Kelly. Ray drove the Camaro into the spring of 1969 before he moved to the Harrell camp. One of Chadwick's crew took over driving until the car was sold later in the year. (Author's Collection)

multi-car shows. At the manufacturers' meet at Orange County late in the year, the Camaro was the only "all Chevy" there. Kelly set the low ET of the meet with a 6.73 and briefly held the title of "World's Fastest Funny Car."

Though Ray Sullins left after 1971 to focus on family and business, he did assist with building Kelly's Vega Funny Car. The Hardy Vega debuted in 1972 and ran with a lot of success through 1974 before its final demise at Union Grove. Tripp Shumake, who had been hired to drive when Kelly moved to Pro Stock, crashed the car after the engine popped a frost plug. The car made a hard right into the path of opponent Connie Kalitta. Though the only injury was to Tripp, who broke a wrist, the $25,000 Vega was lost.

Kelly ran two different Pro Stock Vegas between 1973 and 1975. In 1975, he won a couple points meets and qualified at Indy before he retired. One Vega was wrecked by a later owner and the other is MIA. (Photo Courtesy Gary Anderson)

Just two weeks prior, Kelly had driven the car to a 6.46 at 238 mph on a 75–80 percent load. At the time, this was the fastest times turned by an all-Chevy Funny Car. The loss of the car was a tough one for Chevy fans, as it was the last all-Chevy Funny Car that could compete with the Hemis. The Vega was stripped of what useable parts remained, and the rest was sold as scrap for $15.

Kelly debuted a Don Hardy Pro Stock Vega in 1973 and focused his attention there. He initially ran engines by Carroll Caudle and Booth-Arons, but with a switch to a new car in 1974 came new engines built by his old friend James Gipson. "We built our own engine in the end and ran them with Booth-Arons heads. By the time Kelly was competitive, he had used up all his budget."

Kelly retired in 1975 at the age of 44. His last race was at Odessa, Texas, where he defeated Jenkins's Vega in the final round of an eight-car show. He retired the next day and accepted a coaching job at a high school in Texas. He was immediately inducted into the Division 4 Hall of Fame.

Dick "Mr. Chevrolet" Harrell

As good as Chadwick was, it was Dick Harrell who was bestowed with the title of Mr. Chevrolet. Dick's interest in going fast predates the Korean War and initially centered on the dirt-track jalopies around southern New Mexico. His climb to Mr. Chevrolet status began in 1961 with a Seamist Turquoise 409 Impala. Dressed up to run NHRA Optional/Super Stock with the latest factory goodies, the Impala hit high-12 times by the end of the summer. Dick and his Chevy dominated action across

Dick "Mr. Chevrolet" Harrell was born in Arizona in 1932 and raised on a farm near Carlsbad, New Mexico. His rise to Mr. Chevrolet status began with this car: his second turquoise 1961 Impala. (Photo Courtesy John Bergener/ Bill Fronterhouse)

the Southwest, and stories abound of how he and fellow racer Grady Bryant, who ran a 348-powered Impala, would travel from track to track with Dick's 409 Impala towing Grady's car by chain.

Dick returned in 1962 with a new 409 Impala and captured the NHRA Division 4 points championship. With an aluminum nose on the car, Dick won B/FX at the 1963 NHRA Winternationals. Track owners and promoters took notice of Dick in 1962, and match race dates and appearance money began to roll in. With the help of Morran's Gateway Motors, Dick procured a Z11 Impala, a factory lightweight powered by a 427, in 1963. Dick flat-towed the Impala to the AHRA Winternationals in Arizona, where he cleaned house and defeated the Fords and Mopars to take Top Stock.

Dick enjoyed some factory support during 1962 and into 1963, but when Chevy backpedaled on its racing activities in 1963, Harrell was left to his own devices for the most part. To take on the match race Hemi Mopars and 427-powered Fords, he built himself a Z11-powered Chevelle in 1964. Though it may not be widely known, Dick actually built two Chevelles: one for himself and another near identical car a few months later for a college student named Mack Medley. Mack's father had the resources and helped finance his son's racing activities. The Chevelle was raced mainly around Tucson and Carlsbad, which were tracks close to Cruces, New Mexico, where Mack attended classes. His father warned if school suffered, the car would have to go. Mack's grades suffered in 1965 and his father held true to his word.

Dick debuted his Chevelle early in 1964 and won Street Eliminator at the AHRA Winternationals. That year he carried a new sponsor in the form of Bill Allen Enterprises. Bill worked for, and eventually owned, a Doodle Bug company when Dick first met him back in 1962. Bill bought a single 4-barrel 409 Impala that year and had Dick fine-tune the car. Occasionally, his Impala was seen towing Dick's Impala to the track. Though Bill became disillusioned with the sport in short order, he continued to support Dick with money and his time.

Dick had a phenomenal match race record with his Chevelle and was said to have won 90 percent of the time. He took the car east on tour and proved to be very popular with both racers and fans. When East Coaster Jack Schaffer came calling with hands full of cash and wanted to buy the Chevelle, Dick couldn't say no. Jack sadly wasn't the kind to take real good care of his cars and eventually the much-abused Chevelle burned to the ground.

Harrell's Z11 1963 Impala was preceded by a string of W-motor cars, starting with a 348-powered 1958 in 1959. This Impala was sold to fellow racer Bryan Teal and later wrecked. (Photo Courtesy John Bergener/Bill Fronterhouse)

By mid-1963, Chevy was out of racing. Those who remained loyal to the brand found they could meet and defeat the factory-backed Fords and Mopars by swapping Z11 engines into lightweight Chevelles and Chevy IIs. Dick Harrell built this Chevelle and won his share of national events and match races. (Photo Courtesy John Bergener/Bill Fronterhouse)

And the winner is . . . Dick Harrell. Dick, in the Retribution II, defeated the Chevelle of Mack Medley in Street Eliminator at the AHRA winter meet in 1965. Dick built both cars. (Author's Collection)

Harrell's Chevy II started off as a road racer built by Bill Thomas Race Cars. To get the weight down to a reported 2,300 pounds, plexiglass windows, fiberglass fenders, hood, doors, and decklid were installed. (Photo Courtesy Forrest Bond)

Harrell's match bash Chevy II is nearly ready for paint as it's loaded onto the hauler at Bill Thomas's shop. Drag racing was rapidly evolving in the mid-1960s and cars quickly became obsolete. Nearly every year a new car was required. (Photo Courtesy Troy Criscillis/ Bill Thomas Collection)

Harrell's next ride was a 1962 Chevy II bought from Bill Thomas Race Cars out of Anaheim. Thomas had initially built the Chevy II to run SCCA competition but the car was immediately declared non-production and banned. Under Thomas, the car was dubbed *Bad Bascomb* after an old Western movie and was built with a setback fuel-injected 327 and an independent Corvette rear axle. Once in Harrell's possession, the 327 and independent rear gave way to a 0.060-over Z11 and '57 Pontiac rear end holding 4.56 gears. The Chevy II hit the body shop, where a breakdown in communication resulted in the car being painted black as opposed to the desired red.

The first outing for the Chevy II was the AHRA Winternationals in 1965, where Dick captured the Street Eliminator crown and defeated Medley's Chevelle. Shortly after the winter meet, the *Retribution II* was painted red. To make room for the 10.5 slicks, the quarter panels were "popped-out." This was done delicately by placing a large mine equipment tire inside the wheelwell and inflating it. At some point during the car's evolution, the rear suspension was moved forward and the Z11 gave way to a Mark IV 427. It was a very successful season for Dick and the Deuce, which ran 9s at 140 mph before it met its final demise. It came during an out-of-control, bumper-dragging wheelie. Dick hardly missed a step, and while he waited for his next ride to be completed, he borrowed the *Sad Sac* Chevy II from Tommy McNeely to fill booked dates.

Dick and his deuce were rarely beaten. Here at the famed Lions Dragstrip, he faces the Hemi-powered Skootin 'Cuda *driven by Dr. Richard Spence. Harrell's relationship with Nickey was followed by a deal with Yenko and Fred Gibb. In association with the dealers, Dick built some of the most potent Chevrolet muscle cars of the 1960s. (Photo Courtesy Michael Pottie)*

In debuting his Bill Thomas Race Cars, Nickey Chevrolet-sponsored, 1966 Chevy II, Dick moved to the forefront in the growing altered wheelbase Funny Car scene. The Chevy ran an injected 427 and gulped a 70-percent load of nitro. The potent mill was backed by a 4-speed transmission and a Pontiac rear end stuffed with 4.56 gears. Aiding traction to the 10.5-inch slicks was a 4-inch engine setback and a wheelbase altered by moving the front suspension 3 inches forward and the rear 8 inches forward. The best times noted for the Chevy were an 8.98 at 155.17 mph. It was a great year for Dick; he won a pair of AHRA National events and a countless number of match races.

Mr. Chevrolet's winning ways continued into 1967 with the debut of a Don Hardy Camaro. Built from a body in white, the Camaro retained its steel shell but carried a fiberglass front end, doors, and decklid. Riding on a 2x3 square tube chassis, the body was lengthened 15 inches forward of the firewall and the rear suspension was located 8 inches forward. Dick debuted the car in

the spring with an injected 440. By mid-season, a blower topped the engine and, with up to a 90-percent load of fuel, helped push the 1,800-pound Camaro to 8.50 times at around 175 mph.

The Camaro was sold at the end of the season to make way for a new car, but when the buyer failed to make payment, Dick repossessed the car. How Dick ever found the time to race during this period, I don't know. He campaigned two cars in 1968, with longtime employee Charlie Therwhanger in the 1967 Camaro while Dick drove the new Camaro. Dick's 1968 Camaro was another Don Hardy car and was the first flip-up Funny Car ever built by Hardy.

When the Camaro debuted in 1967, Dick was hired by Nickey to help the dealer build and market 427-powered Camaro muscle cars. According to a *Hemmings* interview with Dick's daughter Valerie, it was through Nickey that Dick met Don Yenko. Dick went to work converting Camaros for Yenko at his dealership in Canonsburg, Pennsylvania. Dick Harrell Performance Center opened around the same time in St. Louis, Illinois.

Bill Thomas Race Cars in So-Cal is where Dick Harrell's match bash Chevy II was built. Initial plans at Bill Thomas were to mass produce these heads-up Chevy IIs. Here Harrell's car is nearly complete. Note the lack of glass and unpainted bumpers. (Photo Courtesy Stephen Justice)

Dick's injected Camaro debuted in the spring of 1967. Don Hardy was responsible for putting the car together, which featured a 2x3 square-tube chassis, a steel body and 'glass bolt-on panels. The red flyer weighed in at a scant 2,300 pounds. To the left is Harrell driver and wrench Charles Therwanger. (Photo Courtesy John Foster Jr.)

Harrell campaigned two near-identical heads-up 1970½ Camaros. He picked up this one from Bill Allen Chevrolet in January 1970 and ran it in AHRA GT-1 and -2 before Harry Kalwei took it over. Harry had been running a 1968 Nova under the Harrell banner, but when the car was wrecked in the fall, Dick suggested he run the Camaro with the Nova's 440-ci engine. The Camaro is pictured here at the NHRA Nationals in 1971, where it was ineligible to run due to its plexiglass windows and lack of front brakes.

Under the hood resides a 509-ci Can-Am aluminum engine that produced a best of 9.64. Harry had the Camaro acid dipped in 1971 and ran it in AHRA Pro Stock through 1973 under the Keep On Tracking sponsor name. (Photo Courtesy Michael Pottie)

When relations with Yenko went south, Dick moved his business to Kansas City. It was while situated in Kansas City that Dick became acquainted with Fred Gibb. Herb Fox, who later drove Dick's 1968 ZL1 Camaro, was driving around Kansas City during the late summer of 1967 and got lost. He pulled into a service station to ask directions and noticed Dick's shop across the street. Herb paid a visit to the shop and suggested to Dick that he talk to his boss, Fred Gibb, up in La Harpe, Illinois, about sponsoring his car. The two met and a sponsor agreement was reached. Part of the deal saw Dick converting Camaros, Novas, and Chevelles to 427 power for the dealer. It was through Fred Gibb that Dick spearheaded the push for Chevrolet to build the ZL1 Camaro in 1969.

Somehow Dick managed to fulfill his business obligations and continued to successfully run a line of

AHRA's man of the decade broke the heart of the Chevy faithful when he switched to Hemi power in 1970. Harrell's success continued until his untimely death in September 1971. (Photo Courtesy Michael Pottie)

drag cars. He can lay claim to being the first to propel a Chevy-powered Funny Car over 200 mph when he hit the mark with his 1968 Camaro during an AHRA Grand American race at Green Valley. Further accolades came for Dick when he was voted AHRA's Man of The Year in 1969 and AHRA's Person of the Decade in 1970. At the close of the decade, Dick and his crew; which included Charlie Therwhanger, Herb Fox, Harry Kalwei, and Ray Sullins; were successfully campaigning Funny Cars, Pro Stocks, and GT cars in AHRA and NHRA competition.

A new Don Hardy Camaro followed in 1971, but along with it came a switch from Chevy power to a Chrysler Hemi. Dick maintained his busy schedule until his untimely death in September 1971 at Toronto, Ontario, while testing tires.

Steve Bovan's Chevy II

Pasadena's Steve Bovan and his 1965 Chevy II showed plenty of promise in the early days of Funny Cars. Bovan purchased this Chevy II new from Jack Wall Chevrolet with a 283 4-speed. With just 69 miles on the odometer, he started the transformation. The car was built at Don Blair's Speed Shop, and foreman Mike Hough performed most of the heavy work, including altering the wheelbase.

The Chevy II was powered by what is believed to be the first blown big-block Chevy on the West Coast. Running straight alcohol, the 2,600-pound Chevy hit a best of 9.29 at 160 mph. Bovan followed with a few Chevy-powered Camaro Funny Cars through 1971, and mainly ran West Coast tracks. By 1977, things had gone sour for Steve. The man who once showed so much promise had gotten involved in the seedy underworld of drugs and the mob. He drew his last breath after being shot in Newport Beach.

Like Chrisman's Comet, *Bovan's Chevy II was forced to run in the Fuel Dragster class in NHRA competition. Steve is caught obliterating the Goodyears at Indy. (Photo Courtesy Forrest Bond)*

Bobby Wood

Bobby Wood may not be as recognized as Chadwick or Harrell, but his Chevys definitely did damage during the heyday of match race Funny Cars. Bobby was born in 1941 and grew up in Birmingham, Alabama. He hailed from a family of entrepreneurs, which included his grandfather who owned Wood Chevrolet in Birmingham for decades. Before he graduated to match race Funny Cars, Bobby knocked them off in the Gasser ranks. He set the C/Gas record in his '55 Chevy with a 12.99 before he moved on to an A/GS 1940 Willys.

In 1965, he took a showroom-fresh Chevelle and turned it into one of the most notorious supercharged match race cars in the nation. Power came by way of a blown stock bore and stroke 396 backed by a B&M Torque-Flite transmission. To aid traction, the Chevelle featured a rear suspension that was moved forward an exaggerated amount. All modification to the car took place at home in Alabama, and that included hanging fiberglass doors, fenders, hood, and trunk lid. Bobby worked extensively with Iskenderian to develop camshafts for the 396 as well as the intake manifold and related parts.

By March 1966, Wood, who seemed to have come out of nowhere, was beating old pros such as the Mustang of Hubert Platt and the *Paper Tiger* Plymouth of Sox & Martin with times in the 9.20s. For Bobby, it got to the point where the Ford and Chrysler reps told their team drivers not to race him.

Julio Marra, track manager and promoter at both Capitol Raceway and Aquasco Speedway, put on his first of 18 annual King of Kings Funny Car shows at Capitol in August. The name for the blown Funny Car Invitational came to him by way of a religious commercial he saw on television. This was the first match bash to feature only blown cars. It was to be an eight-car show that turned into nine when Bobby called to wonder why he didn't get an invite. Julio said, "Bob said he would show up anyway, and if he won, we agreed that I would pay him double the $2,000 win money. I had never heard of Bob and with the likes of Darrell Droke, Jack Chrisman, Ron and Don Gay, Gary Dyer, and Arnie Beswick in the lineup, I figured he didn't stand a chance."

The show opened with Dyer in the Spaulding Dodge defeating Droke's Mustang with an 8.75 time. Next up, Bobby faced the *Kingfish* Barracuda driven by Larry Reyes. Bobby ran an easy 9.33 at 155.17 mph for the win as the Barracuda faltered with transmission ills. Always a crowd favorite, Arnie Beswick set low ET of the meet with a 8.62 in the second round, but in the third he fell to a red light against Bobby's Chevelle. In the final, it was Bobby

She wasn't the prettiest but Bobby Wood and his Chevelle surprised the heck out of a number of top runners. S/FX equated to Supercharged Factory Experimental. Here, Bobby has his work cut out for himself running against Ford/Mercury's best, "Dyno Don" Nicholson. (Author's Collection)

Bobby worked hand in hand with Ed Iskenderian in developing the camshafts, intake, and required parts for the new Mark IV engine. His Chevelles upset many, including Chrysler, who told its factory drivers not to race him. (Author's Collection)

against Gary Dyer. Lady luck shined on Wood this day as the transmission in the Dodge went south after it performed its initial burnout. The 5,000-plus fans watched as Wood soloed for the win.

In 1967, Bobby followed up with what he hoped would be a world-beating 1966 Chevelle powered by a 427. The car lasted just the one season as, according to Bobby, "it didn't handle worth crap." Don Hardy built him a Nova in 1968 for which Bobby built a 500-inch Chevy. He won the AHRA Nationals in Memphis and set

the NHRA record with a 7.61 before he joined the Coca-Cola Funny Car Cavalcade and switched to a Chrysler Hemi in 1970. "The Chevy just couldn't keep the bottom end together as they'd only last three rounds." Bobby retired in 1973 shortly after he defeated Don Schumacher at a '64 Funny Car show in Seattle.

"Jungle Jim" Liberman

For many fans of Funny Cars, the conversation begins and ends with "Jungle Jim" Liberman. The man was a show unto himself, and many track owners benefited immensely by having Jim on the program. Russell James Liberman was born for this sport. He left his home in Pennsylvania during the early 1960s and headed west to the land of endless summers to take up residence in San Jose, where he rented a storage area and converted it into a workshop.

Jim gained drag racing experience behind the wheel of a '57 Chevy that he ran in conjunction with his brother Bob. In 1964, he took the wheel of a Modified Production Chevy II owned by a long-forgotten fellow with the name of Zucovich. In short order the pair swapped an injected, nitro-fed Hemi into *Hercules* and earned a reputation as one of the West Coast's toughest heads-up competitors. Around the same time, Jim befriended local racer Lew Arrington, who, when he wasn't at the track, pulled wrenches at Larry Hopkins Pontiac in San Jose. The pair campaigned a Pontiac-powered Studebaker Lark into early 1965 before they debuted *Brutus*, a blown Hemi-headed Pontiac GTO. It was while driving the GTO that Jim picked up the "Jungle" nickname. As "Jungle Clare" Sanders recalled, "A radio DJ came up with the

Bobby Wood's Supercharged Experimental Stock Chevelle started out as a new, bone-stock Chevelle. With the help of crewmen Paul Love, Joe Freeman, and Bo Winkel, he showed many top names the way home. (Photo Courtesy Michael Cochran)

> **"A radio DJ came up with ['Jungle Jim']
> prior to a match race at Fontana. The
> announcer was doing his high-energy
> routine for a match between Dick Landy
> and Jim. He just blurted it out and it stuck."**
> **– "Jungle Clare" Sanders**

Jim drove the Hercules *Chevy II* in A/MP until 1965, at which point he installed a nitro-burning Hemi for match racing. It was Jim St. Clair who owned the Lime Fire *Barracuda Funny Car*, and his brother who schooled Jim on building nitro engines. (Photo Courtesy Forrest Bond)

Jim Liberman came into his own in 1966 when he debuted this steel-body Chevy II. Liberman fabricated his own chassis and blown 427 for the car. According to Austin Coil, Liberman was the most gifted natural engine builder he'd ever seen. (Photo Courtesy Forrest Bond)

"Jungle Clare" Sanders faces Bill Flynn's Yankee Peddler at Pennsylvania's Numidia Raceway during a summer of 1969 match. The quickest Clare ever ran in the Nova was a 7.53 at 200.44 mph. (Photo Courtesy Carl Rubrecht)

name prior to a match race at Fontana. The announcer was doing his high-energy routine for a match between Dick Landy and Jim. He just blurted it out and it stuck."

Driving for Lew, Jim quickly learned that: one, match racing was where the action and money was; and two, in order to cash in he needed a car of his own. In 1966, Jim built himself an altered wheelbase Chevy II. Powered by a blown 427, the car was built at Richard Guess's Goodies Speed Shop. Taking full advantage of the East Coast's insatiable appetite for match racing, Jim joined Clare Sanders in the *Lime Fire* Barracuda and Don Williamson in the *Hairy Canary* Plymouth and headed east. Jim and company filled tracks across the country

and entertained the fans with 1,000-foot burnouts and wheelstands that put some exhibition cars to shame. Jim ran the 1966 car into 1967 before he called on the Logghe brothers to build him a new chassis to run under a 1967 Chevy II.

By 1968, Jim was ready for a full assault on the masses. He fielded not one but two near-identical Nova Funny Cars. He hired Clare Sanders to run one Nova, which was a new Logghe car carrying Kanuika sponsorship, while Jim ran a Goodies-sponsored Nova that rode on the Logghe chassis from his 1967 Nova. Hired to help keep the Goodies car in tune was Pete Williams, while Larry Petrich lent a hand on the Kanuika car.

At the 1969 NHRA Winternationals, Clare overcame a 32-car field to win the NHRA's first ever Funny Car national event eliminator and defeated the Hemi Barracuda of Ray Alley with a 7.88. Clare recalled that the day after the big win the phone was ringing off the hook with promoters who wanted to book the Jungle cars.

Following the Novas came five different Camaros (seven different bodies, five different chassis) that ran under the Jungle Jim name. Marc Susman, running a Hemi Nova, joined the Jungle Jim team in 1969. The story goes that Jim had plans to switch from Chevy to Hemi power and wanted to gain Hemi experience. Through 1970 and into 1971, his cars carried red paint before Jim made the switch to blue with the swinging "Jungle Jim" caricature. He ran big-block Chevys exclusively before he switched to Hemi power in 1971. Numerous Vegas and Monzas followed, all powered by Chrysler Hemis. He won York US-30s F/C Nationals in 1973 and the Summernationals in 1975, his only NHRA National event that year.

In his later years, Jim's personal life was in shambles a bit. By 1976, trackside attraction "Jungle Pam" Hardy had moved on, and some say just as well. An anonymous source close to Jim stated, "When Jim was still married to Bobbie, she kept him in line and pretty much clean. When she left and Pam showed up, all bets were off and the drugs flowed freely." Jim's untimely death came on the night of September 9, 1977, when his Corvette met a bus head-on.

Doug Thorley

Doug Thorley, the renowned header manufacturer, was another California transplant who came to the Golden State from Utah in the 1940s because, as Doug put it, "It was where drag racing was really happening." His pride and joy was a 1938 Chevy, which was soon followed by a Corvette that he ran at Bonneville. The car was the first C/MS car to break 200 mph. Doug dove into the world of heads-up match racing in 1964 after he made a couple passes in the 427-powered match race Falcon of Hubert Platt. Doug preferred his Chevys and chose a lightweight Chevy II as a starting point.

The Chevy was dubbed *Chevy 2 Much* by Platt's wife who, upon seeing the completed car, exclaimed it was "too much." With its metal flake tangerine paint, the car was a visual knock-out. Adding to the look were relocated front and rear suspensions, a setback engine, and a straight front axle. Doug received some help with the build from M&H and Hilborn but he did most of the work himself at his East L.A. shop. Initial runs in the Deuce were made with a punched-out 283 running Enderle injectors and alcohol.

Once the Mark IV engine became available, Doug made the switch to a Hilborn-injected 396 that propelled the Chevy II to 9-second times at 150 mph. By 1966, his rat motor had been stretched to 482 ci. A 4-speed kept Doug busy in the confines of the aluminum interior while rear drums and a parachute brought the car to a halt. The 98-inch-wheelbase car was initially a handful and went through a number of changes during the couple of years that Doug ran it. One change that aided high-speed stability was the installation of a dropped front axle and lowered rear suspension to get the car out of the air. No one knows how much these changes helped the next owner as he wrecked the car in an on-track crash.

Thorley's Chevy II blasts off on an early morning qualifying run at the 1966 AHRA Winternationals. Born in Cedar City, Utah, Doug moved to the hot rodding hotbed of Southern California in the late 1940s. Doug previously raced everything from flathead Fords to straight-8 Buicks. (Photo Courtesy Forrest Bond)

Doug can take pride in the fact that he won NHRA's first shot at a Funny Car eliminator. It was the 1967 Nationals and Doug was riding high with his 482-ci-powered (4.25 x 4.25) Corvair. The "experts" had all but given the race to the SOHC-powered Mercury Comets, but Doug had ideas of his own and proceeded to lay waste to the competition. I doubt anyone would have ever predicted an all-Chevy final, but that's what they got. Believe it or not, it's the only time two Chevy-powered cars have met in an NHRA national event Funny Car final. In the opposing lane was the Camaro of Joe Lunati. Joe was the lamb on this day, as Doug tripped the lights with a blistering 7.69 at 192.70 mph.

After winning Indy, Doug took up AMC's offer to go racing on the factory dime and built himself a mid-engine Javelin. The Nationals-winning Corvair was sold to the Pisano brothers, who quickly wrecked it. A second Chevy-powered Corvair Doug had went to Dick Bourgeois, who campaigned the car in conjunction with Earl Wade. It was a combination that couldn't lose and rarely did.

The Bourgeois Corvair was rebodied as a Javelin and labeled *Javelin 2*. Bourgeois ran the Coca-Cola circuit in 1969 and won at Irwindale in November with a 7.49 at 193.54 mph to earn the meet's top speed in the process. A 440-ci Chevy propelled the Javelin to a best of 7.38 at 204 mph.

Doug's *Javelin 1* was fairly competitive but never enjoyed the same level of success as his Chevys. The *Javelin 1* was eventually destroyed when it caught air in the lights at Irwindale, which drew to a close the short but sweet drag racing career of Doug Thorley.

Malcolm Durham

The hits kept on coming. Malcolm Durham picked up the nickname "The DC Lip" early in his career as some scribes were reminded of Cassius Clay who carried the nickname "The Louisville Lip." Since Malcolm was black, wasn't afraid to speak his mind, and hailed from Washington DC, the DC Lip moniker seemed a natural fit. Like Clay, Malcolm needled other racers but in a good and funny way and never spiteful.

The DC Lip began his climb in drag racing at North Carolina's Easy Street Dragstrip in a 225-hp '56 Chevy. In 1960, he made the move north to Pennsylvania, where opportunity in the automotive field beckoned. Shortly after, he was off to Washington DC, where he joined the service department at Hicks Chevrolet. By 1962, Malcolm was racing and winning with a 409 Bel Air. The popularity of Malcolm and his Chevy grew around the DC area, and Hicks saw an advantage in moving Malcolm into performance sales. At Hicks, Malcolm befriended salesman Hank Mergner, who busied himself running Corvettes in SCCA competition. Hank employed Malcolm to prepare his 1962 Corvette for action, and it was through Mergner's ties with Chevrolet's Joe Pike that Malcolm received one of the limited Z11 Impalas in 1963.

Malcolm ran A/FX with the 1963, which was the first car to carry the *Strip Blazer* name, and filled his spare weekends match racing the car. For a brief period, he held the A/FX elapsed-time record with an 11.94. In 1964, he ran the car in A/MP and set the MPH record before he swapped the Z11 into a 1964 Chevelle. The Chevelle was a prime example of what might have been had Chevy

With 482 ci, Thorley's Corvair was the baddest in the land. He won NHRA's first Funny Car meet and match raced the heck out of the car, recording 7.30 times. Few could catch him. (Photo Courtesy Lou Hart)

The original Strip Blazer *was an A/MP record holder at 11.24 at 124.40 mph. Today, this ultra-rare Z11 car is restored. Carrying on Malcolm's legacy are his sons Bernard and Bryon. (Photo Courtesy Michael Pottie)*

not reined in its racing activities in 1963.

Malcolm was unable to run his *Strip Blazer* Chevelle in Factory Experimental during 1964 due to the fact NHRA rules dictated that cars running FX had to run current-year engines. At the Nationals, Malcolm was forced to run the car in A/Gas, where he didn't stand a chance against the lighter, blown Willys. Match racing was where the car really shined, as Malcolm captured a reported 90 percent of his bouts. He sure seemed to have Ronnie Sox's number that year. One weekend alone he beat the Sox & Martin Comet seven different times at three different tracks in two different states.

The Chevelle went through a number of changes prior to the 1965 season. The Z11 gave way to an alcohol-injected Mark IV, and 1965 Chevelle body panels were added to give a new-car look. The engine was set back in the chassis 8 inches while the suspension was further altered. Running a dose of nitro saw the Chevelle record 9.50s times before Malcolm retired it.

Looking back, his son Bernard stated, "To Malcolm, the cars were like projects to him. He liked to tinker and

repurpose things. Making them go faster was always the objective." In 1965, Malcolm opened his own business, Race Car Engineering, Maryland, where he served a long list of clients. The name later changed to Supercar Specialties and today is run by Malcolm's son Bryon.

To keep pace in the evolving world of Funny Car, a 1966 Corvair was built for the new season. Malcolm built the chassis in his own shop and ran the car for the next two years. The Corvair became the first Chevy-powered Funny Car to run an 8-second time and did so at a Cecil County match race in August 1966. It was a four-way match between Durham, Del Heinelt in *Seaton's Shaker*, and the hemi cars of Dick Landy and the Ramchargers. Durham topped the tank with 95-percent nitro in hopes of getting around the quicker Ramchargers Dart driven by Mike Buckett. Although Buckett took the win with an 8.63, the attention was all on Durham who recorded an 8.96. Come 1967, the Corvair's wheelbase was stretched from 108 to 118 inches to aid stability and traction, which was hard to find, especially after a 6-71 blower was added to the 427.

You have to love this shot from Dover Dragstrip. Malcolm really gave Sox & Martin fits. This was the second Strip Blazer car. How many Strip Blazer cars were there? Even Malcolm's family isn't sure. (Photo Courtesy Michael Pottie)

Wowing the Fremont crowd was Malcolm Durham and his heavily altered Strip Blazer III Chevelle. The Strip Blazer III was really a modified Strip Blazer II. All modifications to the car were done in-house by Malcolm and company. (Photo Courtesy Steve Reyes)

Malcolm wheeled his new Corvair to a win at the UDRA Nationals held at US-30 in 1966. With the addition of a blower in 1967, the Corvair ran a best of 7.98 at 178 mph. (Photo Courtesy Michael Pottie)

By the late 1960s, the Strip Blazer name was in big demand with promoters and track owners. Malcolm kept them happy with a four-car program. The West Coast's Lee Jones joined Malcolm's team in 1969 with this Firebird/Camaro Funny Car. (Author's Collection)

A Logghe Camaro followed in 1968 and recorded 7.50 times before Malcolm presented drag racing with a four-car show in 1969. Part of his stable were two 427-powered Camaro door cars built to cash in on the match race demand. The *Strip Blazer* name was worth upward of $800 for a best-of-five match. Sharing driving chores on the heads-up Camaros was Roger Butler, who used the *Strip Blazer Jr.* to win the AHRA Summernationals that year. Rounding out the four-car assault was Lee

Jones, who painted his Firebird-come-Camaro in *Strip Blazer* likeness.

Malcolm followed in mid-1970 with a new Camaro Funny Car that made use of the Logghe chassis from his 1968 car. A blower explosion at Aquasco caused the car to be rebodied. A new Gilmore-chassis Camaro followed in 1972. Malcolm ran the 466-ci-powered car through the end of the season before he cut back operations and turned his focus to Pro Stock. Relying upon his own

Strip Blazer Jr. was one of two heads-up Camaros that ran under Malcolm's umbrella in 1969. Both cars were 427-powered, and one was a factory COPO car. (Photo Courtesy Brian Kennedy)

This photo of the Strip Blazer VIII *was made possible by photographer Jeff Tinsley. Jeff got the 12 permits needed to photograph the car next to the reflecting pond across from the capitol building. The Park Service supplied armed guards to keep people clear of the shoot. With its punched-out 454, Malcolm's Camaro was capable of low-7-second times. (Photo Courtesy Steve Reyes)*

This Norman Blake photo catches Durham's Vega at the Summernationals in 1974. The Strip Blazer X was built solely by Malcolm and his crew at his Supercar Engineering shop in DC. (Photo Courtesy Steve Reyes)

Tom Sturm's Chevelle was built off of a showroom SS model and served him into 1966. The relatively stock-looking car is seen here at one of the first, if not the first, Lions booked in match race shows in 1965. The Chevelle ran a reported-best ET of 9.44. (Photo Courtesy Stephen Justice)

abilities and skills, Malcolm built his own small-block-powered Vega at his Supercar Engineering shop. He ran the car in Pro Stock before he switched to Pro Gas in 1977. With the move, the car was rebuilt and a four-link suspension added in place of the ladder-bar setup. The Vega ran well into the 1990s, when it briefly saw action running B/Econo Altered.

There was no quit in Malcolm, whose business continued to thrive in building and fabricating cars for a number of clients. Malcolm took his first retirement from racing in 1985 after he crashed his Don Ness–built, third-generation Pro Stock Camaro. He came back in late 1989 with a nostalgia Pro Mod–style 1965 Chevelle. It was built to run in the 9s, but the nostalgia field he was running with kept getting faster. Arnie Beswick in his Pro Mod–style Pontiac GTO introduced nitro to the mix, which eventually led the group into the 7-second zone. Malcolm finally retired from driving in 2004.

Tom Sturm

Like many early Funny Car pilots, Tom Sturm operated on a shoestring budget. He held down a 9-to-5 at Jardine Headers while running a string of Funnies starting with a Chevelle in 1964. Tom's rise began with a 1962 Bel Air purchased new from Don Steves Chevrolet. A fuel injected Corvette mill powered the car and helped Tom capture the C/FX class at Indy with a 14.71 in 1962, and the NHRA points championship that season. A Z11 Impala in 1963 was followed by a Sachs & Sons–sponsored 427-powered 1963 Mercury Marauder. In 1964, he spent a brief spell in a Jardine-sponsored A/FX Comet before he returned to the Chevy camp and built his *Just 4 Chevy Lovers* Chevelle.

The Chevelle, one of the first altered wheelbase cars on the West Coast, started out as a bone-stock 283-powered Super Sport. As good as the 283 was, there is no way it was going to cut it in the world of big-inch match racers. So out came the little Power Pack and in went a 425-hp 409. A straight axle replaced the A-arm suspension and the wheelbase was slightly altered. A BorgWarner 4-speed was backed by coil spring supported '57 Olds rear mounting fabricated traction arms. At the same time the suspension mods were made, the factory ermine white paint gave way to the more familiar yellow.

The 409 lasted only as long as it took Tom to get his hands on a new-for-1965 425-hp 396. Aftermarket parts for the engine were limited initially, so as driver Larry Reyes recalled, Tom never really tore into it until sometime in 1965. Reyes took the car on a trip back East

Sturm's second Corvair made use of his old Chevelle chassis. The front axle was scavenged from a 1937 Willys, and a '57 Pontiac donated the rear end. Candy tangerine and silver paint made the Corvair a standout. (Photo Courtesy Michael Pottie)

that year, which helped increase Tom's growing fan base. In 1966,, a nitro-fed and -injected 427 measuring 454 inches, thanks to a Crankshaft Co. 4.50 stroke, pushed the Chevelle into the mid-9-second bracket.

Tom had Bill Churchfield behind the wheel of his new *Just 4 Chevy Lovers* Corvair when the car debuted at Lions on April 2, 1966. The debut didn't go quite as planned, as Churchfield stood the Corvair up on its end where it spun into the chain-link fence and came to rest in a near-vertical position. The Corvair ran the injected 427 out of the Chevelle and rode on a Don Hicks square-tube chassis. It was an ill-handling ride that met its demise in June at a match held at Union Hill. Tom closed the season running the Chevelle, which now had the engine mounted behind the windshield.

Tom had better luck with his second Corvair: a Fiberglass Trends flip-up bodied car that mounted on the modified Chevelle chassis. Tom drove the car and also put Dale Armstrong, Tom Mulligan, and Mark Bullet behind the wheel. The engine, now a reported 480 inches, mounted injectors through April before Tom swapped them out for a 6-71 blower. The setup propelled the Corvair into the low-8s.

Sturm debuted his last *Just 4 Chevy Lovers* Corvair late in 1968, which was a blown Don Hardy car that hit 7.60 times. Tom surprised many when he built a Hemi-powered Dodge Challenger in 1970. As a poke at his switch from Chevy to Dodge, he christened the car *The Swapper*. Dale Armstrong drove the car through the season before Tom took over in 1972. That same year, he switched out the Challenger body for a Camaro shell. Tom's later cars were never as popular or successful as his early rides, and he retired after campaigning a second Camaro in 1973.

Bruce Larson

Bruce Larson's drag racing career kicked off in 1954 behind the wheel of a chopped-top 1932 Ford. Bruce remembers the race well, being it was the first East Coast NHRA Safety Safari event that was held in Linden, New Jersey. Bruce was hooked and ran a gambit of drag cars before he built the first all-fiberglass Chevy Funny Car in 1966. He spent 1964 and 1965 dragging a Shelby Cobra with great success. He won multiple NHRA national events including Pomona, Bristol, and Indy; and set class records along the way.

Tom's final Corvair featured a Logghe chassis and Fiberglass Trends body. The 427 now carried a 6-71 blower. Unique to the car was its vinyl-style roof. (Photo Courtesy Michael Pottie)

Larson worked as a mechanic at Sutliff Chevrolet in Harrisburg, Pennsylvania, and raced a Ford. You know changes had to come. Greg Sutliff wised up and realized it was better for his dealership's image if Bruce was behind the wheel of a Chevy, and the ideal choice for the pair was a 1966 Chevelle.

Sutliff managed to wrangle body panels out of Chevrolet before the new cars were released in the fall of 1965 and used them to form fiberglass parts. In typical early Funny Car fashion, the wheelbase of the Chevelle was altered by moving the front wheels forward 4 inches and the rear wheels up 12 inches. Bruce's *USA-1* Chevelle debuted alongside the new Chevys that fall in Sutliff's showroom.

Behind the injected 427 Bruce initially ran a 4-speed, but violent wheelstands and breakage saw him make a switch mid-season to a B&M Turbo-400. The patriotic *USA-1* was tested at Atco, New Jersey, prior to being towed to California to participate in the NHRA Winternationals. In one of its first matches on a cold March 27th at Island Dragway, Bruce defeated the *Flying Carpet*, the 1965 Dodge of Bob Harrop. With Harrop's Hemi on nitro and the Chevelle on alcohol, Bruce took the match with a best of 10.20. By the end of the season, the Chevelle was recording 9.40 times.

The Chevelle was updated in 1967 with new panels and ran a best of 8.78. In March, Bruce hung an extra couple hundred pounds on the Chevelle and won the 2,600-pound Funny Car Eliminator at the Bakersfield March Meet.

Having wrung out all he could from the Chevelle, Bruce debuted a B&N fiberglass Camaro in 1968. Bruce called on the Logghe brothers to build the 118-wheelbase, Stage 1 chassis that housed a blown, stock-inch 427. The Camaro posted an all-time best ET of 7.41 at the 1968 Super Stock Nationals. At the time, it was the lowest ET ever turned by a Funny Car.

In 1969, the 2,000-pound Camaro earned Bruce Funny Car honors at the Super Stock Nationals and a semifinal-round appearance at Indy. Bruce ran the Camaro through 1969 before he debuted the first second-generation Camaro Funny Car. The new Fiberglass Ltd Camaro featured the Logghe chassis from Bruce's 1968 Camaro. The much-trusted 427 filled the rails.

Taking advantage of NHRA rules, Bruce had a new "mini" Camaro built in 1971 that featured a Logghe Stage II chassis. A switch from his trusted iron-block 427 in mid-1972 to a hemi ended in disaster when he split the crank. The ensuing fire saw the car burn to the ground. Bruce stepped away from Funny Cars at that point and tried his hand in Pro Stock.

"I could see Grumpy Jenkins was having a lot more fun with a lot fewer problems with his Vega Pro Stocker so I thought I'd try that for a while." Bruce rented Grump's 1970 Camaro and had it labeled in his familiar *USA-1*

Bruce Larson made a name for himself by campaigning a multinational-event-winning Shelby Cobra in 1964–1965, but he's best remembered for his string of winning Chevy Funny Cars. The Chevelle was the first of the fiberglass cars to debut, having been completed in the fall of 1965. (Photo Courtesy Dean Johnson)

Bruce and Sutliff Chevrolet presented an appealing show. Everything was first class from the Funny Car through to the tow car. Bruce ran a similar outfit into the 1970s, updating the Funny Car and tow car to a second-gen Camaro. (Photo Courtesy Carl Rubrecht)

Bruce's 1970½ Camaro was the first second-gen Camaro Funny Car to debut. When asked of the origins of the USA-1 moniker, Bruce stated, "We heard that Chevrolet was going to use USA-1, depicting number one in sales for an advertising slogan." This rendition of the USA-1 ran 7.10s at more than 200 mph. (Photo Courtesy Bruce Larson)

colors. At the same time, Bruce placed an order with SRD Race Cars for a Vega of his own. Though the Camaro seemed outdated running legal Pro Stock, Bruce had no problem winning some match races against Ronnie Sox and Don Nicholson with his big-inch Jenkins Mountain Motor.

Bruce built his own engines for the Vega with some guidance from Jenkins and Booth-Arons. As with all SRD cars built at the time, the Vega featured a wishbone style three-link rear suspension, a setup that Bruce never really

got sorted out. When the opportunity arose to buy a Don Hardy Vega (with its four-link suspension) at the beginning of the 1974 season, Bruce took it. In the end, things never really worked out for Bruce in Pro Stock. From the perspective of a Funny Car pilot he stated, "I have a lot of respect for the Pro Stock drivers. The cars are harder to drive, harder to work on, don't sound right, and don't smell right."

The Vega was sold at the end of the 1974 season and Bruce headed back to the Funnies. His efforts culminated

The stock-inch 427 featured all the top goodies 1970 had to offer: Venolia pistons swinging on good Chevy rods, a Crane cam, and a Donovan-supplied 6-71 blower. Backing the motor was a B&M-prepared Turbo-Hydra-Matic. (Photo Courtesy Michael Pottie)

Bruce Larson debuted his SRD Pro Stock Vega at the NHRA Springnationals in 1973. Booth-Arons heads topped small-blocks of various sizes. The Vega was sold to Bob Ingles when Bruce returned to Funny Car racing. (Photo Courtesy Ed Aigner)

Pete Seaton's original **Seaton's Shaker** was this 1964 Chevelle, updated with a 1965 fiberglass front clip. To improve traction, the body was set back on the chassis and the engine was relocated. (Photo Courtesy James Handy)

in an NHRA World Championship title in 1989 while he competed against the likes of Bernstein, Force, and Prudhomme.

Seaton and Hedrick

This is a story of two men: Pete Seaton, son of a GM big wig; and Terry Hedrick, a Californian who found fame by moving to Michigan. Terry, a mechanic by trade, had been turning wrenches for the Herrera brothers on their Willys Gasser and working a 9-to-5 at Doug Thorley's header shop. He helped Doug with building and maintaining his *Chevy 2 Much* and took it out on tour with him. Along the way he met Pete Seaton, and when he had a falling out of sorts with Thorley, Terry made the move east. He worked a stint with Chevrolet before he hooked up with Jay Howell and lent a hand at his chassis shop. It was through Howell that Hedrick met Pete Seaton. Seaton loved his drag racing, but a rare blood disease kept him out of the driver's seat.

His first *Seaton's Shaker* was a 1965 Chevelle that was initially powered by an injected 396. As the new-for-1965 Mark IV Chevy predated the availability of speed equipment, Seaton adapted 427 Ford Hilborn injectors to the 396. Driving chores were left up to business partner Jim Cornell and wrench man Del Heinelt.

By the end of 1965, a 427 had replaced the 396 and Seaton billed the Chevelle as the world's fastest Chevy, which clocked 9.40 times on a 65-percent load of nitro. According to draglist.com, the body was mounted 7 inches back and 1 inch higher on the chassis. With fiberglass fenders, doors, hood, decklid, and bumpers, the Chevelle weighed in at 2,800 pounds. A lot of work went into setting up the suspension as a means of planting the 10-inch slicks. This may explain the cars tendency to perform tremendous wheelstands. The Chevelle was wrecked during a match race against the Ramchargers at Detroit in May 1966. With a roll cage made from exhaust tubing,

Terry Hedrick leased his name to Don Peulecke, who campaigned this 427 Camaro in 1972. The Chicago-based Camaro ran mid- to high-9-second times. Terry retired from driving in 1973 after he crashed his Hemi-powered Dodge Colt. (Photo Courtesy John Foster Jr.)

Del Heinelt was the lucky one to man the controls of Pete Seaton's storming 1966 Chevelle. The body was slid back 7 inches on the modified chassis and the nitro-injected 427 was positioned rearward an equal amount. (Photo Courtesy Ed Aigner)

it's surprising driver Del Heinelt walked away. In short order, a 1966 Chevelle body was swapped onto the chassis. Del moved on to other pastures and Jay Howell came on board to take his place.

Jay's Automotive Engineering set to work on building Seaton's first of three Corvairs in 1966, a car that ripped off 8-second times with an injected big-block. Primitive by today's standards, the latest *Seaton's Shaker* had a steel body with fiberglass panels and a tube chassis. Jay briefly drove the car and, with a blower added, dove further into the 8s. By the spring of 1967, Terry Hedrick was the regular driver.

A new Logghe car was built for 1968 that featured a 118-inch wheelbase and a flip-up Fiberglass Trends body. Reported best times were in the 7.30s at 204 mph. Hedrick became the new owner of the Corvair in 1968, when

Pete dropped out of racing. It seems Pete's new wife didn't care for drag racing and, according to Terry, "She didn't care much for me either." In 1969, the Corvair body was replaced with a Nova body. The *Super Shaker* clocked a 6.97 early in 1970 to become the first Chevy-powered Funny Car to run in the 6s. The Nova body was lost due to a blower explosion and replaced with a 1971 Camaro shell. Terry lost that one in a fire and spent a couple months laid up recouping from burns. I hate to say it, but the Chevy motor was replaced with a Hemi when a new *Super Shaker* Vega was built. Terry's final go-around was with an outlaw Hemi-powered Colt driven by Paul Sullivan. After crashing the ill-handling beast, Terry retired.

Terry Hedrick was the owner of Seaton's Shaker Corvair by the time this photo was taken in 1968. The Corvair shell was wrecked and replaced with a Nova body for 1969. Check out the Phony Pony in the background; a stretched fiberglass Mustang on a slingshot chassis. (Author's Collection)

Hedrick's Nova featured a Fiberglass Trends shell and a 118-inch-wheelbase Logghe chassis. Unique to the Nova was its independent front suspension. Times of 7.20s in 1969 made the Nova one of the most-feared Chevys in the nation. (Photo Courtesy John Foster Jr.)

Fred Totten's *King Camaro*

The *King Camaro* of Fred Totten, based in Phoenix, Arizona, was a unique piece. Not because of its Exhibition Engineering chassis or the colorful Nat Quick paint, but because of its Dean LaPole twin plugs per cylinder, big-block Chevy. The additional eight plugs were tapped into aluminum plates that were sandwiched between the block and heads. The plates created a large open combustion chamber and a booming exhaust note. The 427 used both front- and rear-mounted distributors to fire the 16 plugs. To this day, the Camaro holds the record for the fastest Chevy-powered Funny Car. In 1972, LaPole drove the car to a 6.40 at 228 mph time.

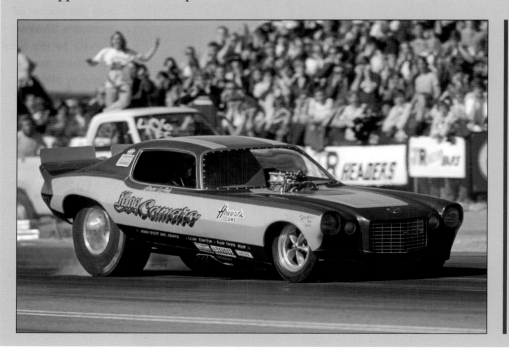

Fred Totten's Arizona-based King Camaro, seen here at Scottsdale, Arizona, featured an Exhibition Engineering chassis and colorful paint by the famed Nat Quick. The Camaro ran a Dean LaPole twin plugs per cylinder, big-block Chevy. The eight additional spark plugs were tapped into aluminum plates sandwiched between the block and heads. To this day, the Camaro holds the record for the fastest Chevy-powered Funny Car, which LaPole drove to 6.40 at 228 mph in 1973. (Photo Courtesy Steve Reyes)

☆☆☆ *THE BEST OF THE REST* ☆☆☆

By the time the 1970s rolled around, replica fiberglass Chevy bodies were pretty much all that remained of the manufacturer in the category. The Hemi ruled, using aftermarket blocks by Ed Donovan and Keith Black that led the charge. A few drivers struggled on with their Chevys, but the writing was on the wall.

Ric Deschner was the last of a breed when he campaigned this big-block-powered AA/FC Monza in 1985. He ran the car into the early 1990s, recording a best of 6.50 at 218 mph in 1978 on a 45-percent load. These are considered the fastest times turned for a cast-iron Chevy Funny Car. The colorful paint was laid by famed painter Circus. (Photo Courtesy Allen Tracy)

Ric Deschner was an independent in every sense of the word and did it all himself, including building his 427 engines and fabricating his own chassis. With no sponsor and no budget, Ric still managed to do what few of the megadollar operations were doing at the time, and that was having fun on his own dime. (Photo Courtesy Allen Tracy)

☆☆☆ *THE BEST OF THE REST* ☆☆☆

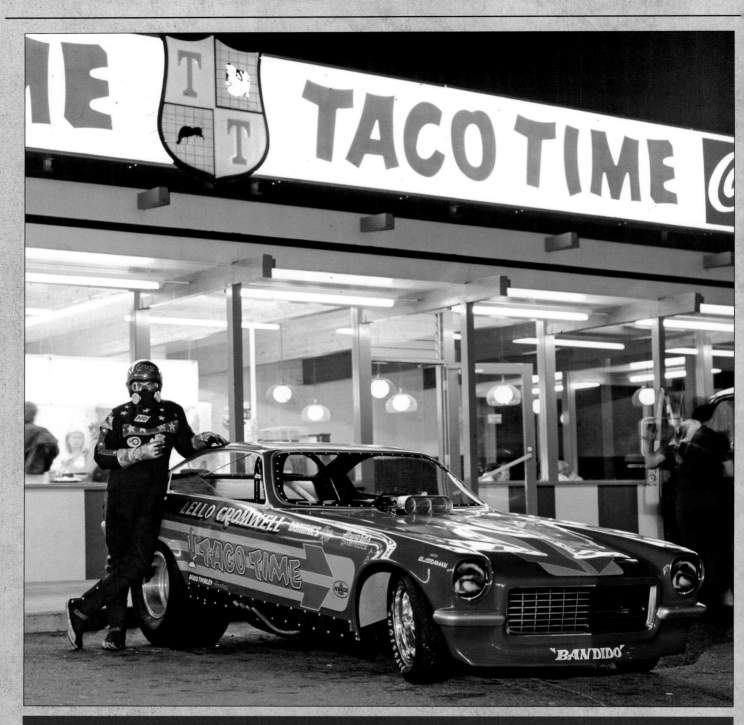

This 1971 photo of Joe Colello's Chevy-powered Taco Time Vega was shot by Steve Reyes. Colello, whose family owned a chain of grocery stores in the Northwest, offered to fly Steve up to shoot the car at a local Taco Time. Gary Cromwell drove and worked on that car and also a Chevy-powered AA/FD. Taco Time was thrilled with its Popular Hot Rodding cover, and so were Colello and Cromwell. Gary Cromwell has the Vega and plans to restore it. (Photo Courtesy Steve Reyes)

This Blountville, Tennessee, A/Dragster beauty, seen at Indy in 1961, was owned and driven by Ronnie Cox and wrenched by Willard Gott. The Chevy between the Lynwood Chassis rails featured a front-mounted 6-71 blower using Potvin equipment and a Joe Hunt magneto to keep it in competition. (Author's Collection)

Chapter Seven

Off the Rails

There's no point in kidding ourselves. When it came to the Dragsters, be they Top Fuel, the old AA/Fuel and BB/Fuel, Chevy-powered cars for the most part took a back seat to the hemi-headed Chryslers. From the 1950s through to today, the Hemi or its aftermarket derivatives have pretty much owned the dragster classes. Contrary to what some may believe, the hemispherical combustion chamber is not a Chrysler invention. The design first appeared around 1900 in Europe and had been used by a few manufacturers before Chrysler adopted the design in 1951. Up until that point, Ford's flathead and earlier OHV engines reigned supreme.

Ollie Morris

Chevy's V-8 first made an impression in 1955 when Ollie Morris snuck one into his rear-engined *White Owl*. Built using 1929 Model A rails wrapped in a fabricated aluminum shell, Ollie initially ran a 275-ci Ford midship. In 1954, he joined forces with Fred Offenhauser, who at the time was doing some work for Chevrolet. Fred received three 265 engines from Chevy, one of which replaced the flathead in *Ollie's Smokin' White Owl*. As the aftermarket for the new Chevy mill was pretty much nonexistent at that point, the pair went about to develop their own parts and farm out work to companies such as Jahns to forge their pistons, and Potvin to ground their camshafts. Stu Hilborn made one of his first (if not the first) Chevy fuel injections for the engine.

At the inaugural NHRA Nationals at Great Bend, Kansas, in 1955, Ollie went undefeated in Top Eliminator and clocked a best of 141.28 mph on a 95–98 percent load of nitromethane. The race came down to the final

The clone of the White Owl *is spot on to the original flathead Ford. Ollie soon realized the flathead was done and replaced it with a 265 Chevy. Dan Marvin, Ollie's grandson, started the build with Ollie before the legendary racer passed in 2008. (Photo Courtesy Tom West/ Lou Hart Collection)*

four before rain brought the proceedings to a halt. When the race picked up again, two months later in Arizona, Offenhauser didn't want to pay to have the car shipped there, so Ollie never showed.

Chester "Chet" Herbert

Hot on Ollie's heels was Chester "Chet" Herbert. Chet is probably better remembered for his camshafts than for his on-track endeavors. His interest in going fast dates back to the 1940s and initially focused on motorcycles. Though stricken with polio in 1948 and left paralyzed from the waist down, Chet refused to allow the disease to slow him down. His ongoing efforts culminated in the building of *The Beast*, a 90-cc Harley that clocked 129 mph at Santa Ana in 1950.

Chet's early automotive efforts included a Chevy six he built for a circle-track racer that incorporated a roller cam of Chet's own design, which was an industry first that helped the engine produce 275 hp. In the late 1950s, he perfected the twin inline Chevy dragster and teamed with Zane Shubert to win AA/FD at the 1961 AHRA Winter Nationals held at Green Valley, Texas. Chet assembled the twin small-block Chevys that were supplied to him direct from Zora Arkus-Duntov. The bore and stroke of each was said to be 4.25 x 4.0 to give 454 inches.

When it came to the unorthodox in dragster design, Chet came up with some of the best. How about a pair of rear-mounted sidewinder Chevys? Chet tried to pull it off in 1961 with twin 454-ci Chevys connected via 3

flywheels, 52 clutch disks, and a pair of spider gears with the rear engine running the wheels. The ill-handling AA/FD measured 120 inches in length and proved more than a handful for driver Zane Shubert. The car clocked speeds in the mid-160s, when it could be kept on the straight and narrow.

Chet took a break from the unusual in 1963 when he and Shubert built a single engine slingshot. He returned to the twin-engine design in 1967 with Beebe & Ayer's twin-blown 400-inch Chevy rail and the beautifully enclosed *Pulsator* of Nye Frank.

The *Pulsator* morphed into the Herbert-LaBarron slingshot in 1971. It was powered by twin 402-ci tunnel-

Another Chet Herbert-Zane Shubert invention was this ill-handling twin sidewinder. The car never did follow the A to B principle and was shelved. You can file this one under the chapter, "What were they thinking?" (Author's Collection)

rammed and injected Chevys that were joined front to front as opposed to the usual back to front. According to *Hot Rod* magazine, "The two engines were joined by incorporating a one-and-a-half-inch adapter. The cranks were welded together, and welded to the adapter was a single steel sprocket for gear drive. Both camshafts ran off of one center gear drive." The cam in the front engine was ground backward to run in reverse. Firing the engines evenly was a single 16-plug distributor. With something like 1,800 hp on tap, the goal of hitting 200 mph seemed realistic. If it ever made it, it was never reported.

"Sneaky Pete" Robinson

At the 1961 NHRA Nationals, "Sneaky Pete" Robinson and his 352-ci Chevy-powered AA/FD turned more than a few heads. Off the trailer his blown and injected Chevy unleashed low ET of the day with an astounding 8.68 time. It left many questioning the accuracy of the clocks, even those in the tower who refused to share Pete's recorded time. Funny, nobody seemed to have an issue with the clocks when Tom McEwen in the McEwen and Adams 475-inch blown Olds rail laid down a 9.01 at 170.45 mph.

Pete commented, "I was pretty burned because they wouldn't show me my times for two days, but they weighed me five times." Jack Hart eventually had no choice but to relent as follow-up runs produced similar ETs. Pete opened up Sunday's eliminations with an 8.52 and proceeded to trailer Jack Chrisman and Eddie Hill on his way to a final round meeting with McEwen. It was a close race up until about half-track when Robinson began

> **"I had gone through something like five engines that year and had only been out of state once. I was pretty much unknown when we headed to Indy with junk, and I mean junk."**
> **– "Sneaky Pete" Robinson**

to inch ahead. Across the line it was Robinson's Chevy with an 8.86 at 170.77 mph to McEwen's 8.90 at 168.55.

In an interview back in the day, Pete recounted that he had blown his engine about a week prior to the 1961 Nationals. "I had gone through something like five engines that year and had only been out of state once. I was pretty much unknown when we headed to Indy with junk, and I mean junk." Not only had Pete won Indy with a junk engine, he had only been in the 8s once prior to the Nationals, which happened during a match at Brooksville, Florida.

Always the innovator, Pete didn't earn the "Sneaky Pete" nickname for no reason. Prior to the 1963 running of the NHRA Nationals, Pete installed a jacking system on his AA/Dragster. Trying to get one up on the competition, Pete staged his car, raised the rear, and spun the tires at approximately half throttle. When the light turned green, he dropped the rear and got the jump on his competition. Although nothing in the rule book said the jacks were illegal, after he set a low ET with an 8.50, the NHRA director Ed Eaton quickly banned their use. Pete's last go in a Chevy rail was in 1964. Toward the close of the season, Ford made him an offer that he couldn't refuse and he jumped ship.

Chet Herbert and Zane Shubert's last venture together was this 402-ci (1-inch stroke 283) Chevy-powered rail in 1965. Referred to as "The Chevy," it was one that regularly had its way with the Hemis. It was one of the first Chevy-powered rails to break 200 mph. (Photo Courtesy Forrest Bond)

"Sneaky Pete" Robinson's Chevy-powered rail walked off with Top Eliminator at the 1961 Nationals and defeated Tom McEwen in the final. Robinson had a low ET of the meet with an 8.68 time. The chassis was a Dragmaster tweaked by Pete. (Author's Collection)

Freight Train

When talking Top Gas Dragsters, the *Freight Train* of John Peters and Nye Frank has to be at the top of the list. It all but owned the category in the 1960s. In total, there were three *Freight Train* dragsters and all were powered by twin-blown small-block Chevys. The first was built in 1959 and featured a single front-mounted 6-71 blower that fed both engines through one long intake duct. Peters quickly picked up on the advantage of running twin blowers, and in short order, each engine housed its own. The blowers were connected via a shaft that had the front blower running the rear blower.

The car continued to evolve, and in 1962 it picked up its first major win and grabbed Top Gas at Bakersfield while being driven by the infamous Bob Muravez, a.k.a. Floyd Lippencotte Jr. Through the 1960s, Floyd captured an ungodly number of class wins and six national event titles. In 1967, he set the class record at a UDRA meet at Lions with a 7.31 at 200.44 mph. History has recorded this as the first 200 mph blast by a Top Gas car.

The *Freight Train*'s list of accomplishments is long: It was the first Top Gas car to break 190, the first to run a 7-second time, and the first to run a 6-second time. Peter's team won the Division 7 points championship five times, and in 1967 were low qualifiers at every meet they ran.

The last *Freight Train* was built in 1968. In 1970, John partnered with Walt Rhodes and the small-block Chevys gave way to a pair of Chrysler Hemis.

Drag News *columnist Judy Thompson gave John Peters's rail the* Freight Train *name in the early 1960s after watching it defeat the competition by a train's length. Driver Bob Muravez made over 1,300 runs in the car, and at one point went 28 consecutive rounds without a loss. (Photo Courtesy Forrest Bond)*

Hemi Hunter

The Division 1–based *Hemi Hunter* Top Fueler debuted in 1969 and did a superb job in living up to its name. Campaigned by Jim Johnson, Gary Peters, Danny Rausch, and Wayne McCollough, and driven by Dale Thierer through 1972, the car won the division points championship in 1971 and accumulated 2,800 points. It was the last Chevy-powered Top Fuel car to win a division title. Relying upon a tall deck Chevy and a number of factory parts, including steel heads and an L88 crank, the *Hemi Hunter* earned the title of the fastest Chevy in 1972 by recording 6.50 times. Other goodies that made the Chevy run included Arias pistons, Howards rods, and a flat-tappet cam. A 95-percent load of fuel flowed through the largest pump they could find and filled the cylinders through 16 nozzles. Topping the Bower blower was an Enderle bug catcher. Behind the Chevy was a Crower clutch and direct drive to a Chrysler 8¾ rear end.

A rear-engine S&W *Hemi Hunter* was built in 1974, but by then the aftermarket hemis had proved their dominance. New faces Mike Duffy and Howard Haight joined the team and though they did well in the face of the hemi onslaught, they were never able to match the success of the previous car. The rear-engine *Hemi Hunter* was retired in 1980.

*Caught here melting the hides at Maple Grove, Dale Thierer wheeled the **Hemi Hunter** to the Division 1 points championship in 1971. The 205-inch chassis was built by S&W. (Photo Courtesy Michael Pottie)*

Leo Dunn

By the mid-1970s, the hemi was the only way to go if you wanted to win in *any* dragster category. Leo Dunn and his twin Chevy-powered AA/D was one exception to the unwritten rule when he won Pro Comp at the 1975 NHRA Springnationals. Leo kicked off his drag racing career 22 years earlier behind the wheel of a 1948 Chevy and ran a number of Chevy-powered Gassers and a Comp Coupe before he built his first of three twin-engine rails in 1967. The dragster was powered by injected small-blocks that carried Jim through 1968 before he debuted his twin big-block-powered car in 1969. Sharing the driving chores with Leo in the new car was Bob Drummond.

Leo's most successful car was his third twin-engine that was built in 1971 by Jim Davis, who was one of the gentlemen who shared the driving of Leo's first twin-engine car. Jim fabricated the 248-inch chassis that housed rear-mounted injected aluminum 427s. Joe Ortega drove the AA/Dragster between 1974 and 1980 brought Leo his biggest win when he recorded a 7.15 at 192.30 mph to defeat Ken Veney's hemi Vega to win the 1975 Springnationals. The car's best times came at the March Meet in 1981 where Larry Sutton drove it to a 6.80 on alcohol.

In 1981–1982, Larry drove the car in AA/DA before it was retired. Leo took the car apart and for years it sat in storage with Rich Burnelli, Leo's partner in all the twin cars. Rich, among countless others, had the honor of restoring the car in 2017 for Leo's daughter, Vickie.

Rich Brunelli owned Central Chevrolet and was Leo's 50/50 partner on all the twin-engine dragsters. The engines were connected at the crank by a double chain. (Photo Courtesy Vickie Dunn)

The best years ended with the twin Chevys and the last gasp for the *Freight Train* was a win at the 1971 Gatornationals. When the NHRA killed Top Gas at the end of the 1971 season, Peters chose to retire.

Jim Bucher

In 1975, Jim Bucher of West Chester, Ohio, found himself on a short list of those running a big-block Chevy in Top Fuel. He bucked all odds with his aging rail and won the year's NHRA Summernationals. It was one of the last national victories for Chevy in Top Fuel.

Jim was a graduate of Top Gas and can take credit for earning the category's last national event win with his twin Chevy–powered slingshot. Against the screams of "Save Top Gas," the NHRA unceremoniously killed the category at the end of the 1971 season. At the season-closing Supernationals, Jim was declared the winner over the hemi-powered mid-engine car of Ken Ellis. Though Ken crossed the line first, he was later disqualified for running too light.

Jim's Top Fuel car debuted in 1973 and was built around a 225-inch Stebbins chassis. The mid-engine dragster housed a 468-inch aluminum Chevy that fed on an 80-percent load. Filling out the mill were Howards cam and rods, a 30-percent-over Danekas blower, and a Mallory ignition. In a sea of Ed Pink and Keith Black after-

Built in 1972, the best time turned for Bucher's Chevy was a 5.91 at 248 mph recorded at Ontario in 1975. Jim's go-fast secret was light weight. He went to extremes to get the car down to its reported 1,200 pounds. (Photo Courtesy Allen Tracy)

market Hemis, Jim's rail opened eyes after it set the Top Fuel record at the Gatornationals in 1973 with a 6.079 at 236.22 mph. Jim made it to the final round, where his hopes were dashed when he broke against Herm Petersen.

He appeared at the rain-delayed 1975 Summernationals with a crew of Henry Wernke, Dale Galter, and his three brothers Mike, Tim, and Rick in tow. The 468 was humming and ran consistent mid-6s on a bad track. In the final, Jim faced Gary Beck and took the win with a 6.50 time. It was hard to believe but this was Chevy's first Top Fuel win since Pete Robinson did the deed at the Nationals back in 1961. The car made it to the finals once more, this time at the Gatornationals in 1976, where Jim fell to James Warren.

"Save Top Gas" went out the cry to no avail in 1971. Jim Bucher's twin Chevy took Top Gas honors at the last event of the year, the Supernationals, where he defeated the twin-Hemi car of Ken Ellis. (Photo Courtesy Steve Reyes)

A new Larry Paye car came in 1976 and showed a lot of potential before Jim was forced into retirement. Today, the car resides in the Don Garlits museum. (Photo Courtesy Larry Pfister)

Jim built a new Larry Paye car for 1976 and debuted it mid-season. Reportedly some 150 pounds lighter than the Stebbins car, the Paye rail never reached its full potential before Jim fell ill and passed away. Many were left wondering what could have been.

Lidtke-Zeller

The last pure Chevy Top Fuel car to win an NHRA national event belonged to Dwayne Lidtke and Ray Zeller. With Stan Shiroma at the helm, the team's Kenny Ellis–chassis dragster took the win at the 1977 Fallnationals. The feat was accomplished with a factory tall-deck block and steel open-chamber heads. Ray was responsible for building the engines and set out from the get-go to prove that a Chevy could live on nitro.

"When I got into the partnership with Dwayne, Chevy had a very bad reputation for tossing blowers, which I thought was stupid." Ray felt the issue had more to do with the tuning and nothing to do with it being a Chevrolet.

As Ray recalled, "We used parts that were pretty generic for the time that proved very reliable. The car required very little maintenance." Ray called Keith Black a mentor, followed his lead, and ran low, 6:1 compression in the engine. Helping the Chevy

run high-5 times were a 4.125 stroke and a flat-tappet cam cut by Jack Engle. The engine ran an enormous amount of ignition timing, 84 degrees enormous, and all the fuel pump they could "beg, borrow, or steal." The weak link, if there was one, was that on occasion they would lose a block, breaking the deck at the head studs. The car ran faster than Ray ever thought it would and stated he couldn't give a particular reason why. "It surprised all of us," he said.

At the Fallnationals, Stan qualified number 10 with a 6.00 ET and had to defeat number-two qualifier Frank Bradley in the first, James Warren in the second, and Ernie Fall in the third to face the Rodeck-powered *Valley Fever* car of Rance McDaniel. As luck would have it, Rance failed to fire, which allowed Stan to single for the win. With the Rodeck being an aftermarket Chevy block, this is also considered the last all-Chevy Top Fuel final.

The guys ran the car for a couple more years and incorporated a Rodeck block toward the end of 1979. The car ran no better with the new engine, though it may have been more reliable.

Seen here in 1977, the Dwayne Lidtke and Ray Zeller Chevy Top Fueler hailed from Los Angeles and was driven by Stan Shiroma. The team later switched from a Chevy cast block to a 481 Rodeck in front of a 2-speed. The car had 4.30 rear gears. (Photo Courtesy Larry Pfister)

✰✰✰ *THE BEST OF THE REST* ✰✰✰

Facing the Chrysler Hemi and Cammer Fords, Chevy really had no place in the Top Eliminator category. However, it held its own—be it briefly—thanks to a high-revving small-block and lightweight chassis. When it came to Top Gas and the Junior Dragster categories, it was a different story, and there was plenty to cheer about.

Lefty Muderbach, in the Howard Cam Special, opened the 1961 season by taking Top Eliminator at the AHRA winter meet with a record time of 8.63. At the AHRA Nationals that year, Lefty took AA/GD while Zane (left) won AA/FD with his twin 454-ci Chevys. Top eliminator was run among top class winners, and neither had any competition in the twin-engined classes, so they automatically went to the finals in Top Gas and Top Eliminator. (Photo Courtesy Forrest Bond)

This rear-engine Chevy rail was built by Bill and Dave Coleman of Elk Ridge, Maryland. The brothers ran the car from 1959 to 1961, and at one time it was considered the World's Fastest Chevy and clocked 8.70s at 180 mph in September 1961. (Author's Collection)

A/Dragster was no home for the W-motor, but Jerry Gitthens, seen here at Oklahoma's Mar Car Dragway in 1963, saw some success with the 409. Jerry took class at the 1964 NHRA Winternationals. (Photo Courtesy Joe Gitthens)

The 1957–1963 NHRA nitro ban led to Dragmaster building the Two Thing in 1960. Tom Nelson was responsible for building the twin 354-ci engines that were meshed at the flywheel with the left engine running reverse. The Two Thing set the top speed at the 1960 NHRA Nationals at a little over 171 mph and won best engineered car. A return to Indy in 1961 saw the team set top speed at 177.87 mph. (Author's Collection)

Not that you have to go back to 1961 for a Chevy dragster win, but at the Nationals that year, Hildardo "Hill" Alcala in Dean Moon's A/D took class. The 301-ci Chevy was good for low 9-second times. The chassis was built by Dragmaster. (Author's Collection)

John Rodeck proved his aluminum Chevy block could survive in the world of Top Fuel. The short-wheelbase car is caught in action at the World Finals in 1974. (Photo Courtesy Stephen Justice)

The first 25 years sure set the bar for years to come. But you know there will always be those who step up to the bat. The following years have shown us this in everything from Pro Stock to Stock. How can we forget the careers of Pro Stock legends Jim Yates, Greg Anderson, or Jeg Coughlin Jr.? And then there's Erica Enders, the first lady of Pro Stock, who won a pair of world Championships behind the wheel of a Chevy in 2014 and 2015.

Today Factory Stock has picked up where yesterday's Pro Stock left off. Running 7.70 times, the cars have more in common with earlier Pro Stocks than just quarter mile times; for one, these limited-production cars actually retain their assembly-line looks. Like Pro Stock of yesteryears, these racers have their work cut out for them with Ford's Mustang and the Dodge Challenger proving to be more than game.

In Super Stock, I could easily mention a dozen different cars, but let's go with Dan Fletcher. His 1968 Camaro is the winningest car in NHRA history. As of this writing, Dan has 104 national event wins and 3 World Championships, and no doubt with more to come from the Fletcher family.

Stay tuned folks. The future looks bright for the Chevrolet racer with countless more victories and world titles to come.

Dan Fletcher's Camaro has been a drag car from day one. Dan's father, Taylor, initially ran it in Modified. Following in his father's footsteps, Dan entered the world of drag racing in the 1980s. (Photo Courtesy Lou Hart)

Additional books that may interest you...

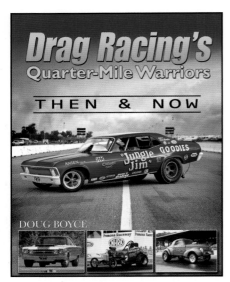

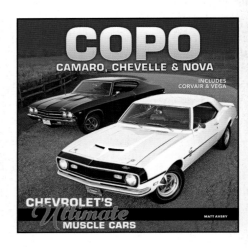
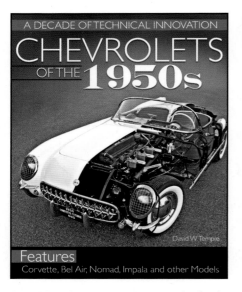